Social Choice with
Partial Knowledge of
Treatment Response

Social Choice with Partial Knowledge of Treatment Response

IS A PART OF THE SERIES

ECONOMETRIC INSTITUTE LECTURES

Series Editors

Herman K. van Dijk and Philip Hans Franses

The Econometric Institute, Erasmus University Rotterdam

The *Econometric Institute Lectures* series is a joint project of Princeton University Press and the Econometric Institute at Erasmus University Rotterdam.

This series collects the lectures of leading researchers which they have given at the Econometric Institute for an audience of academics and students.

The lectures are at a high academic level and deal with topics that have important policy implications. The series covers a wide range of topics in econometrics. It is not confined to any one area or sub-discipline.

The Econometric Institute is the leading research center in econometrics and management science in the Netherlands. The Institute was founded in 1956 by Jan Tinbergen and Henri Theil, with Theil being its first director. The Institute has received worldwide recognition with an advanced training program for various degrees in econometrics.

The first volume in this series is *Social Choice with Partial Knowledge of Treatment Response* by Charles F. Manski.

Social Choice with Partial Knowledge of Treatment Response

Charles F. Manski

Princeton University Press
Princeton and Oxford

Library of Congress Cataloguing-in-Publication Data

Manski, Charles F.
 Social choice with partial knowledge of treatment response /
Charles F. Manski
  p. cm. - (The Econometric Institute Lectures)
 Includes bibliographical references.
 ISBN 0-691-12153-2 (cl: alk. paper)
 1. Social sciences—Statistical methods. 2. Social choice.
 3. Estimation theory. I. Title. II. Series.

HA29.M2466 2006
300′.1′5195—dc22   2005048691

British Library Cataloguing-in-Publication Data

A catalogue record for this book is available
from the British Library

This book has been composed in Computer Modern and
typeset by T&T Productions Ltd, London

Printed on acid-free paper ∞
www.pup.princeton.edu

Printed in the United States of America

10 9 8 7 6 5 4 3 2 1

Contents

Preface

This monograph codifies and elaborates the Econometric Institute and Princeton University Press (PUP) Lectures that I presented at Erasmus University Rotterdam in June 2004. I am grateful to the Econometric Institute, to PUP, and especially to Herman van Dijk for this opportunity to unify and further develop a program of research that I began in the late 1990s and continue today. I am grateful to Adam Rosen for his careful reading of the manuscript and to several anonymous reviewers for their comments. The National Science Foundation supported this work through grant no. SES-0314312.

Chapter 1 is a largely verbal, and I hope broadly accessible, development of basic themes. Chapters 2–4 are necessarily more technical, but empirical illustrations and numerical examples aim to help one interpret the math. I feel that the analysis in these chapters answers some important questions. Nevertheless, I anticipate that readers will conclude, as I do, that the study of social choice with partial knowledge of treatment response is barely beyond its infancy. I shall be pleased if publication of this book stimulates new research that broadens and deepens the present analysis.

Social Choice with Partial Knowledge of Treatment Response

1
Utilitarian Treatment of Heterogeneous Populations

1.1 Studying Treatment Response to Inform Treatment Choice

An important practical objective of empirical studies of treatment response is to provide decision makers with information useful in choosing treatments. Often the decision maker is a planner who must choose treatments for a heterogeneous population. In the utilitarian tradition of welfare economics, the planner may want to choose treatments whose outcomes maximize the welfare of this population.

Consider, for example, a physician choosing medical treatments for a population of patients. The physician may observe each patient's demographic attributes, medical history, and the results of diagnostic tests. He may then choose a treatment rule that makes treatment a function of these covariates. If the physician acts on behalf of his patients, the outcome of interest may measure his patients' health status, and welfare may measure health status minus the cost of treatment, in comparable units.

Or consider a judge choosing sentences for a population of convicted offenders. The judge may observe each offender's past criminal record, demeanor in court, and other attributes. Subject to legislated sentencing guidelines, she may consider these covariates when choosing sentences. If the judge acts on behalf of society, the outcome of interest may measure recidivism, and social welfare may decrease with recidivism and the cost of carrying out a sentence.

Empirical studies of treatment response are useful to physicians, judges, and other planners, to the extent that they reveal how outcomes vary with treatments and observable covariates. There are fundamental, practical, and volitional reasons why studies of treatment response do not provide all the information that planners would like to have. An obvious but fundamental reason is that outcomes can be observed only for treatments that have already been received. Hence, a planner cannot know prospectively how persons will respond to alternative treatments. Moreover, observation of treatment response in a study population that has previously been treated can at most reveal the outcomes that these persons experienced under the treatments that they actually received. The counterfactual outcomes that members of the study population would have experienced under other treatments are logically unobservable.

Practical problems of data collection enlarge the gap between the information that planners would like to have and the evidence that empirical studies of treatment response provide. The mundane fact that data collection is costly may constrain researchers to study small samples of survey respondents or experimental subjects. Planners may want to learn long-term outcomes of treatments, whereas studies of treatment response may only measure short-term outcomes. Survey respondents may refuse to answer or may respond inaccurately to questions about the treatments that they have received and the outcomes that they have experienced. Experimental subjects may not comply with assigned treatments or may drop out of trials before their outcomes are measured.

The volitional reasons are the researchers' choices that limit the usefulness of their work to planners. Much empirical research on treatment response tests hypotheses that bear only a remote relationship to the treatment choice problems that planners face. Researchers frequently study populations that differ substantially from those that planners treat. Researchers rarely report how treatment response varies with the covariates that planners observe. Research findings often rest on untenable assumptions. See Section 1.3 for further discussion.

To learn how studies of treatment response can be most helpful to planners, I find it productive to eliminate the distinction between researcher and decision maker. That is, I maintain the perspective of a planner who can perform his own research in the service of treatment choice. The planner observes a study population, combines this empirical evidence on treatment response with assumptions that he deems credible, and then chooses treatments for the population of interest. This monograph examines how a planner may reasonably go about this task.

1.2   The Planning Problem

To move beyond generalities, it is necessary to pose the treatment choice problem that I shall presume a planner faces. As in Manski (2000, 2001, 2002, 2003, Chapter 7, 2004, 2005), I assume that a planner must choose treatments for the members of a heterogeneous population. Each member of the population has a response function that maps treatments into an outcome of interest.

The planner may observe some covariates that differentiate members of the population. The observed covariates determine the set of treatment rules that are feasible to implement. These are functions that map the observed covariates into a treatment allocation.

I assume that the planner wants to choose a treatment rule that maximizes population mean welfare; that is, he wants to maximize a utilitarian social welfare function. This problem has a simple solution—the optimal treatment rule assigns to each member of the population a treatment that maximizes mean welfare conditional on the person's observed covariates. However, the planner does not have all the knowledge of treatment response needed to implement the optimal rule. What the planner does have is the ability to observe a study population in which treatments have already been selected and outcomes have been realized. The planner's problem is to use the available empirical evidence and credible assumptions to make treatment choices.

1.2.1   The Choice Set

To formalize the planning problem, suppose that there is a finite set T of mutually exclusive and exhaustive treatments. Each member j of the treatment population, denoted J^*, has a response function $y_j(\cdot) : T \to Y$ mapping treatments $t \in T$ into outcomes $y_j(t) \in Y$. The planner is concerned with the distribution of outcomes across the population, not with the outcomes of particular persons. Hence, it is convenient to make the population a probability space (J^*, Ω, P). Then the probability distribution $P[y(\cdot)]$ of the random function $y(\cdot) : T \to Y$ describes treatment response across the population.

A planner must choose a treatment rule assigning a treatment to each member of J^*. A fully specified treatment rule is a function $\tau(\cdot) : J \to T$ that assigns a treatment to each person. Person j's outcome under rule $\tau(\cdot)$ is $y_j[\tau(j)]$. I assume that treatment is individualistic; that is, a person's outcome may depend on the treatment he is assigned, but not on the treatments assigned to others.

The planner observes certain covariates $x_j \in X$ for each member of the population; thus, $x : J \to X$ is the random variable mapping persons into their observable covariates. To simplify analysis, I suppose that the covariate space X is finite and that $P(x = \xi) > 0$, $\forall \xi \in X$. The planner can differentiate persons with different observed covariates, but cannot distinguish among persons with the same observed covariates. Hence, a feasible treatment rule is a function that assigns all persons with the same observed covariates to one treatment or, more generally, a function that randomly allocates such persons across the different treatments.

Formally, let Z denote the space of functions that map $T \times X$ into the unit interval and that satisfy the adding-up conditions: $z(\cdot, \cdot) \in Z \Rightarrow \sum_{t \in T} z(t, \xi) = 1$, $\forall \xi \in X$. Then the feasible treatment rules are the elements of Z. An important subclass of Z are the *singleton* rules that assign all persons with the same observed covariates to one treatment; that is, $z(\cdot, \cdot)$ is a singleton rule if, for each $\xi \in X$, $z(t, \xi) = 1$ for some $t \in T$ and $z(s, \xi) = 0$ for all $s \neq t$. Nonsingleton rules randomly allocate persons with covariates ξ across multiple treatments, with assignment shares $[z(t, \xi), t \in T]$. This definition of nonsingleton rules does not specify which persons with covariates x receive each treatment, only the assignment shares. Designation of the particular persons receiving each treatment is immaterial because assignment is random and the planner's objective is to maximize population mean welfare.

In some settings, a planner may not be permitted to use certain covariates (say race or gender) to assign treatments. If so, the present description of the choice set remains accurate if x is defined to be the covariates that the planner is permitted to use, rather than the full vector of covariates that the planner observes.

1.2.2 The Objective Function and the Optimal Treatment Rule

The planner wants to choose a feasible treatment rule that maximizes population mean welfare. The welfare from assigning treatment t to person j is

$$u_j(t) \equiv u[y_j(t), t, x_j],$$

where $u(\cdot, \cdot, \cdot) : Y \times T \times X \to R$ is the welfare function. The planner knows the form of $u(\cdot, \cdot, \cdot)$ and observes x_j. However, he does not observe the potential treatment outcomes $[y_j(t), \ t \in T]$.

Welfare may, for example, have the additive "benefit–cost" form

$$u[y(t), t, x] = y(t) + c(t, x),$$

where $c(t, x)$ is the real-valued cost of assigning treatment t to a person with covariates x, and $y(t)$ is the real-valued benefit of this treatment. In the case of a physician, $y_j(t)$ may measure the health status of patient j following receipt of treatment t, and $c(t, x_j)$ may be the (negative-valued) cost of treatment. At the time of treatment choice, the physician may know the costs of alternative medical treatments but not their health outcomes. Similarly, in the case of a judge, $y_j(t)$ may measure the criminal behavior of offender j following receipt of sentence t, and $c(t, x_j)$ may be the cost of carrying out the sentence. Again, the judge may know the costs of alternative sentences but not their criminality outcomes.

For each feasible treatment rule z, the population mean welfare that would be realized if the planner were to choose rule z is

$$U(z, P) \equiv \sum_{\xi \in X} P(x = \xi) \sum_{t \in T} z(t, \xi) E[u(t) \mid x = \xi]. \quad (1.1)$$

The planner wants to solve the problem

$$\max_{z \in Z} U(z, P). \quad (1.2)$$

Let S denote the unit simplex in $R^{|T|}$. The maximum in (1.2) is achieved if, for each $\xi \in X$, the planner chooses the treatment allocation $z(\cdot, \xi)$ to solve the problem

$$\max_{z(\cdot, \xi) \in S} \sum_{t \in T} z(t, \xi) E[u(t) \mid x = \xi]. \quad (1.3)$$

The maximum in (1.3) is achieved by a singleton rule that allocates all persons with covariates ξ to a treatment that solves the problem

$$\max_{t \in T} E[u(t) \mid x = \xi]. \quad (1.4)$$

There is a unique optimal rule if problem (1.4) has a unique solution for every $\xi \in X$. There are multiple optimal rules if (1.4) has multiple solutions for some $\xi \in X$. In the latter case, all rules that randomly allocate persons with the same covariates among their optimal treatments are optimal. In any event, the population mean welfare achieved by an optimal rule is

$$U^*(P) \equiv \sum_{\xi \in X} P(x = \xi) \left\{ \max_{t \in T} E[u(t) \mid x = \xi] \right\}. \quad (1.5)$$

1.2.3 The Value of Covariate Information

The population welfare achievable by an optimal treatment rule depends on the observed covariates. The set of feasible treatment rules grows as more covariates that differentiate members of the population are observed. Hence, the optimal welfare cannot fall, and may rise, as more covariates are observed.

In particular, compare $U^*(P)$ with the welfare achievable when no covariates are observed. In that case, the optimal feasible treatment rule yields welfare $U^0(P) \equiv \max_{t \in T} E[u(t)]$. Hence, the value of observing covariates x is the nonnegative quantity $U^*(P) - U^0(P)$. If observation of x is costly and welfare is measured in commensurate units, $U^*(P) - U^0(P)$ is the amount that the planner should be willing to pay to observe x.

The value of observing x is positive whenever optimal treatments vary with x. It is zero if there exists a common optimal treatment, that is, a t^* that solves (1.4) for all values of x. Thus, observable heterogeneity in treatment response is relevant to treatment choice if and only if optimal treatments vary with the observed covariates.

1.2.4 *Partial Knowledge of Treatment Response*

A planner who knows the treatment-response distributions $P[y(t) \mid x]$, $t \in T$, can choose an optimal treatment rule. Economic theorists studying social choice have long assumed that planners know the response distributions and have sought to characterize the resulting optimal treatment rules. See, for example, Mirrlees (1971) on optimal income taxation, Polinsky and Shavell (1979) on optimal fines, and Shavell and Weiss (1979) on optimal unemployment benefits.

My concern is a planner who does not know the response distributions but who can observe a study population in which treatments have been selected and outcomes realized. I consider how such a planner may use the available empirical evidence and credible assumptions to choose treatments reasonably.

If observation of a study population is to yield information useful in treatment choice, a planner must be able to extrapolate from the study population to the treatment population. With this in mind, I assume that the study population, denoted J, is identical in distribution to the treatment population J^*. Thus, J is a probability space whose probability measure P is the same as that of J^*. The only difference between J and J^* is that some *status quo treatment rule* has already been applied and outcomes experienced in the former population, whereas a treatment rule is yet to be chosen in the latter.

It is often optimistic to suppose that a planner can observe a study population that is distributionally identical to the treatment population. Nevertheless, treatment choice is a formidable task even in this benign setting. I focus on two ubiquitous problems. First, outcomes are observable only for the treatments that members of the study population received under the status quo treatment rule; the outcomes of counterfactual treatments are necessarily unobservable (Chapter 2). Second, outcomes may be observed only for a random sample drawn from the study population, in which case the planner must perform statistical inference from this sample to the population (Chapters 3 and 4).

While the chapters ahead differ in their specification of the available empirical evidence, they all ask how a planner with partial knowledge of treatment response may reasonably make treatment choices. Decision theorists have studied various criteria for decision-making with partial information, but no consensus prescription has emerged and it may be that none will ever emerge. I apply the Wald (1950) development of statistical decision theory and, within Wald's framework, I focus most attention on the minimax-regret criterion proposed by Savage (1951). The minimax-regret criterion is appealing in principle and yields treatment rules that seem quite reasonable in the applications that I have studied. Nevertheless, I do not assert that a planner with partial knowledge of treatment response should necessarily make treatment choices in this way. I discuss other criteria as well.

1.2.5 Nonseparable Planning Problems

An important property of the optimal treatment rule (1.4) is that it is separable across covariate values. That is, the optimal rule for persons with covariates ξ is invariant with respect to the situations of persons with other values of x. This separability, which greatly simplifies analysis of treatment choice, rests on three assumptions: the planner is utilitarian, the set of feasible treatments is rectangular, and treatment is individualistic. To close this section, I call attention to important planning problems that do not satisfy separability and that, consequently, are not studied here.

Nonutilitarian Objective Functions

The idea of a planner with a utilitarian social welfare function carries forward a long tradition in public economics. Nevertheless, I would not assert that the utilitarian perspective is necessarily realistic in all settings. Analysis of treatment choice from nonutilitarian perspectives would be welcome, but is beyond the scope of this monograph. Nonutilitarian objective functions generically make social welfare depend on the relative positions of different members of the population. A consequence is that optimal nonutilitarian treatment rules are not generally separable across covariate values.

Nonrectangular Sets of Feasible Treatment Rules

I assume that the set of feasible treatment rules is rectangular; that is, the set of treatments that are jointly feasible to assign across the population are the Cartesian products of the treatments that are feasible to assign to each member of the population. Budgetary or technological constraints may render a treatment set nonrectangular, in which case optimal treatment rules generally are not separable.

Suppose, for example, that there is a budgetary upper bound on the total cost of treating the population. Then the feasible treatment rules satisfy the inequality

$$\sum_{\xi \in X} P(x = \xi) \sum_{t \in T} z(t, \xi) c(t, \xi) \leqslant K,$$

where K is the budget and $c(t, \xi)$ is the cost of assigning treatment t to a person with covariates ξ. The budget constraint binds if the total cost of the optimal rules determined in (1.4) exceeds K. If so, application of (1.4) is infeasible.

Social Interactions

Individualistic treatment means that each person's outcome depends only on the treatment that he is assigned, not on the treatments assigned to others. Social interactions occur when personal outcomes do depend on the treatments assigned to others. The present analysis does not cover problems of treatment choice with social interactions.

1.3 Practices that Limit the Usefulness of Research on Treatment Response

In Section 1.1, I stated four ways in which choices made by researchers studying treatment response often limit the usefulness of their work to planners. Having posed the planning problem, I can now elaborate.

1.3.1 Hypothesis Testing

Empirical research on treatment response has been strongly influenced by the classical theory of hypothesis testing, especially by the idea of testing the null hypothesis of zero average treatment effect; that is, equality of $E[y(t)]$ and $E[y(t')]$ for specified treatments t and t'. This null hypothesis is prominent in experimental design, where researchers use norms for statistical power to choose sample sizes. Research findings may go unreported or may be deemed to be "insignificant" if they do not meet test-based criteria for statistical precision.

Hypothesis testing has been particularly influential in medical research using randomized clinical trials. A standard reference on the design and analysis of clinical trials gives this prescription for choice of sample size in a trial (Meinert 1986, p. 74): "With a sample size calculation, the investigator sets out to determine the number of patients required to detect a designated treatment difference with specified levels of type I and type II error protection." Many medical researchers (e.g. Halpern, Karlawish, and Berlin 2002) consider it unethical to conduct "underpowered" trials, in which the sample size does not make the probability of a type II error sufficiently small, given a specified value for the probability of a type I error. Testing the hypothesis of zero average treatment effect is institutionalized in the US Food and Drug Administration (FDA) drug approval process, which calls for comparison of a new treatment under study $(t = b)$ with a placebo or an approved treatment $(t = a)$. FDA approval of the new treatment normally requires rejection of the null hypothesis of zero average treatment effect $\{H_0 : E[y(b)] = E[y(a)]\}$ in two independent clinical trials (Fisher and Moyé 1999).

Hypothesis testing is remote from treatment choice. The classical practice of handling the null and alternative hypotheses asymmetrically, fixing the probability of a type I error, and seeking to minimize the probability of a type II error, makes no sense from the perspective of treatment choice. Moreover, error probabilities at most measure the chance of choosing a suboptimal rule; they do not measure the damage resulting from a suboptimal choice. For these and other reasons, research reporting the results of hypothesis tests yields little information of use to a planner.

1.3.2 The Study Population and the Treatment Population

Much research on treatment response downplays the importance of correspondence between the study population and the population to be treated. Donald Campbell argued that studies of treatment effects should be judged primarily by their *internal validity* and only secondarily by their *external validity* (e.g. Campbell and Stanley 1963; Campbell 1984). By internal validity, Campbell meant the credibility of findings within the study population, whatever it may be. By external validity, he meant the credibility of extrapolating findings from the study population to another population of interest.

Rosenbaum (1999, p. 263) recommends that observational studies of human subjects aim to approximate the conditions of laboratory experiments:

> In a well-conducted laboratory experiment one of the rarest of things happens: The effects caused by treatments are seen with clarity. Observational studies of the effects of treatments on human populations lack this level of control but the goal is the same. Broad theories are examined in narrow, focused, controlled circumstances.

Rosenbaum, like Campbell, downplays the importance of having the study population be similar to the population of interest, writing (Rosenbaum 1999, p. 259): "Studies of samples that are representative of populations may be quite useful in describing those populations, but may be ill-suited to inferences about treatment effects."

In accord with Campbell and Rosenbaum, many researchers concerned with the evaluation of social programs analyze treatment response in easy-to-study populations that differ fundamentally from the populations that planners must treat. A common practice has been to report the "effect of treatment on the treated," where "the treated" are the members of a study population who actually received a specified treatment (see, for example, Bloom 1984; Angrist 1990; Gueron and Pauly 1991; Dubin and Rivers 1993). Attempting to cope with the problem of noncompliance in randomized experiments, Imbens and Angrist (1994) and Angrist, Imbens, and Rubin (1996) recommend that treatment effects be reported for the subpopulation of "compliers," these being persons who would comply with their designated experimental treatments whatever they might be.

From the perspective of treatment choice, analysis of treatment response in an easy-to-study population is sensible if treatment response is homogeneous. Then planners can be confident that research findings can be extrapolated to the populations they must treat. In human populations, however, homogeneity of treatment response may be the exception rather than the rule. Whether the context be medical, educational or social, it is reasonable to think that persons vary in their response to treatment. To the degree that treatment response is heterogeneous, a planner must take care when extrapolating research findings from a study population to a treatment population, as optimal treatments in the two may differ. Hence, correspondence between the study population and the treatment population assumes considerable importance.

1.3.3 Reporting Observable Variation in Treatment Response

To inform treatment choice, research on treatment response should aim to learn how treatment response varies with covariates that planners can observe. If all persons respond to treatment in the same manner, then it is best to treat all persons uniformly. However, if treatment response varies with observable covariates, then planners can do better by implementing treatment rules in which treatment varies appropriately with these covariates. For example, judges may be able to lower recidivism among criminal offenders by sentencing some offenders to prison and others to probation. Social workers may be able to increase the life-cycle earnings of welfare recipients by placing some in job training and others in basic skills classes. In these and many other cases, the key to success is determining which persons should receive which treatments.

Nevertheless, the prevalent research practice has been to report treatment response in the population as a whole or within broad subpopulations, rather than conditional on the covariates that planners may observe. An article reviewing evaluations of training programs for the economically disadvantaged exemplifies the problem (Friedlander, Greenberg, and Robins 1997). Throughout their extended discussion of inferential problems that arise in evaluating training programs, the authors assume that all potential trainees respond uniformly to treatment. Their subsequent discussion of empirical findings presents separate estimates of treatment effects only for the very broad demographic groups of adult men, adult women, and youth. The authors do not, even in their concluding "Agenda for Future Evaluations," ask how response to training may vary with schooling, work experience, or other covariates that the administrators of training programs may observe.

The Friedlander et al. article faithfully portrays the literature that it reviews, so I do not intend to single it out for criticism. Similar inattention to observable heterogeneity in treatment response is prevalent in other major literatures. Consider the vast body of medical research through clinical trials. Physicians commonly have much information—medical histories, diagnostic test findings, and demographic attributes—about the patients they treat. Yet the medical journal articles that report on clinical trials typically present estimates of treatment effects aggregated to broad demographic groups.

An article on a clinical trial comparing alternative psychosocial treatments for cocaine dependence provides an apt illustration. Crits-Christoph et al. (1999) report on a National Institute on Drug Abuse study randomly placing 487 cocaine-dependent patients in one of four treatment groups, each designated treatment combining group drug counseling (GDC) with another form of therapy. In some respects, the article is attentive to the possibility of heterogeneity in treatment response. The authors call attention to the fact that previous findings on the relative merits of psychotherapy and drug counseling for treatment of opiate-dependent patients do not hold up in the context of cocaine dependence. They provide much descriptive information on the characteristics of the subjects, including measures of race, sex, age, education, employment status, type and severity of drug use, psychiatric state, and personality. They test hypotheses that treatment effects do not vary with patient psychiatric state or personality. However, the article does not report outcomes conditional on any of the patient covariates observed by the researchers. Indeed, its formal "Conclusion" section makes no reference to the possibility that treatment response might vary with observable covariates, stating simply (Crits-Christoph et al. 1999, p. 493): "Compared with professional psychotherapy, a manual-guided combination of intensive individual drug counseling and GDC has promise for the treatment of cocaine dependence."

Why have researchers done so little to analyze observable heterogeneity in treatment response? Some researchers may firmly believe that, in their study settings, treatment response is homogeneous across the population. If so, then covariate information has no value. However, it is difficult to imagine many cases in which it is credible to assume homogeneous treatment response, without empirical investigation.

I conjecture that the primary reason why researchers neglect to analyze observable heterogeneity in treatment response is concern for the statistical precision of their estimates of treatment effects. (I can only conjecture this because researchers rarely state explicit reasons for what they do not do.) As discussed above, conventional ideas about what constitutes adequate statistical precision for an empirical finding to be of interest have been strongly influenced by the theory of hypothesis testing. Conditioning on covariates generally reduces the statistical precision of estimates of treatment effects, often to the point where findings are "statistically insignificant" by conventional criteria. Hence, researchers often restrict their attention to estimation of population-wide average treatment effects, or effects within major subpopulations such as adult women or youth.

Chapter 3 will show that, if researchers wish to inform treatment choice, they should not view statistical insignificance as a reason to refrain from studying observable heterogeneity in treatment response. A planner must be concerned with the quantitative variation of outcomes with treatments and covariates. Hypothesis tests simply do not address this question.

1.3.4   Untenable Assumptions

Powerful incentives often influence researchers studying treatment response to maintain assumptions far stronger than they can persuasively defend, in order to draw strong conclusions. The scientific community tends to reward those who produce unambiguous findings. The public, impatient for solutions to its pressing concerns, tends to reward those who offer simple analyses leading to unequivocal policy recommendations.

Especially commonplace has been research using untenable assumptions to infer the outcomes that members of study populations would have experienced under counterfactual treatments. Heckman and Robb (1985) provide a compendium of assumptions that logically suffice to infer counterfactual outcomes from data on observed outcomes. However, researchers applying these assumptions are rarely able to provide much substantive justification for them.

Research findings based on untenable assumptions are not much use to a planner facing the treatment choice problem of Section 1.2. The objective of such a planner is to maximize *actual* social welfare, not the social welfare that would prevail if untenable assumptions were to hold.

2

The Selection Problem

All research on treatment response confronts a fundamental problem of missing outcome data, commonly known as the *selection problem*. Treatments are mutually exclusive, so one cannot observe the outcomes that a person would experience under all treatments. At most, one can observe the outcome that a person experiences under the treatment he or she actually receives. The counterfactual outcomes that would have been experienced under other treatments are logically unobservable.

Suppose, for example, that patients ill with a specified disease can be treated by drugs or by surgery. The objective may be to predict the life spans that would occur if patients with specified risk factors were to receive each treatment. The available data may be observations of the actual life spans of the patients in a study population, some of whom were treated by drugs and the rest by surgery. The life spans that patients who received drug treatment would have experienced with surgical treatment are unobservable.

Formally, let $s(\cdot) : J \to T$ denote the status quo treatment rule applied in the study population. Each person $j \in J$ realizes treatment $s(j)$ and outcome $y_j \equiv y_j[s(j)]$. Person j does not experience the treatments $(t \neq s(j))$; hence, $y_j(t)$, $t \neq s(j)$, are counterfactual outcomes. I assume throughout this chapter that a planner observes the (covariate, treatment, outcome) triples (x, s, y) of all members of the study population. Hence, the planner learns the distribution $P(x, s, y)$. However, knowledge of $P(x, s, y)$ only partly identifies the response distributions $P[y(t) \mid x]$, $t \in T$.

To cope with the selection problem, researchers routinely combine available data with assumptions that are sufficiently informative about counterfactual outcomes as to point identify the distribution of treatment response. The assumptions imposed seldom possess a secure foundation and often have no basis at all. Consequently, planners and other readers of research on treatment response frequently do not know what to make of reported findings.

I think it preferable to first consider how a planner who knows nothing about counterfactual outcomes might make treatment choices. This is the subject of Section 2.1, which builds on Manski (2000, 2002). In Sections 2.2 and 2.3 I study assumptions about counterfactual outcomes that may sometimes be credible enough for a planner to impose them with confidence.

2.1 Treatment Choice Using the Empirical Evidence Alone

What does knowledge of $P(x, s, y)$ reveal about the distribution of treatment response? As shown in Manski (1990, 1995), the answer follows quickly from the equation

$$
\begin{aligned}
P[y(t) \mid x = \xi] \\
= P[y(t) \mid x = \xi, \ s = t]P(s = t \mid x = \xi) \\
+ P[y(t) \mid x = \xi, \ s \neq t]P(s \neq t \mid x = \xi) \\
= P(y \mid x = \xi, \ s = t)P(s = t \mid x = \xi) \\
+ P[y(t) \mid x = \xi, \ s \neq t]P(s \neq t \mid x = \xi), \quad (2.1)
\end{aligned}
$$

which holds for each $\xi \in X$. The first equality is the Law of Total Probability. The second holds because $y(t) = y$ for persons who receive treatment t.

Knowledge of $P(x, s, y)$ reveals $P(y \mid x = \xi, \ s = t)$, $P(s = t \mid x = \xi)$, and $P(s \neq t \mid x = \xi)$, but is uninformative about $P[y(t) \mid x = \xi, \ s \neq t]$. Hence, the *identification region* for $P[y(t) \mid x = \xi]$ using the empirical evidence alone is the set of distributions

$$H\{P[y(t) \mid x = \xi]\}$$
$$= \{P(y \mid x = \xi, \ s = t)P(s = t \mid x = \xi)$$
$$+ \gamma P(s \neq t \mid x = \xi), \ \gamma \in \Gamma_Y\}, \quad (2.2)$$

where Γ_Y denotes the space of all probability distributions on Y. Moreover, the identification region for the vector of outcome distributions $\{P[y(t) \mid x = \xi], \ (t, \xi) \in T \times X\}$ is the Cartesian product

$$H\{P[y(t) \mid x = \xi], \ (t, \xi) \in T \times X\}$$

$$= \mathop{\times}_{(t,\xi) \in T \times X} H\{P[y(t) \mid x = \xi]\}. \quad (2.3)$$

This holds because knowledge of $P(x, s, y)$ is uninformative about the vector of counterfactual distributions $\{P[y(t) \mid x = \xi, \ s \neq t], \ (t, \xi) \in T \times X\}$, which can take any value in $\times_{(t,\xi) \in T \times X} \Gamma_Y$.

Inspection of equation (2.2) shows that observation of the study population is increasingly informative for $P[y(t) \mid x = \xi]$ as the prevalence of counterfactual outcomes falls. At one extreme, $H\{P[y(t) \mid x = \xi]\} = \Gamma_Y$ if $P(s \neq t \mid x = \xi) = 1$; thus, the study population is uninformative about $P[y(t) \mid x = \xi]$ if the status quo treatment rule assigned no one with covariates ξ to treatment t. At the other extreme, $H\{P[y(t) \mid x = \xi]\} = P(y \mid x = \xi, \ s = t)$ if $P(s \neq t \mid x = \xi) = 0$; thus, the study population reveals $P[y(t) \mid x = \xi]$ if the status quo rule assigned everyone with covariates ξ to treatment t. It is important to keep in mind that as $P(s \neq t \mid x = \xi)$ falls, the prevalence of counterfactual outcomes for other treatments commensurately rises. This tension is a fundamental feature of the selection problem.

2.1.1 Ambiguity in the Ranking of Treatment Rules

Now consider treatment choice using the empirical evidence alone. Let Γ index the set of feasible states of nature. Thus, $(P_\gamma, \; \gamma \in \Gamma)$ is the set of values for P that are feasible given the planner's knowledge of $P(x, s, y)$. Let $z \in Z$ and $z' \in Z$ be any two feasible treatment rules. Rule z is said to *weakly dominate* z' if $U(z, P_\gamma) \geqslant U(z', P_\gamma)$ for all $\gamma \in \Gamma$ and $U(z, P_\gamma) > U(z', P_\gamma)$ for some $\gamma \in \Gamma$. The ranking of the two rules is ambiguous if $U(z, P_\gamma) > U(z', P_\gamma)$ for some $\gamma \in \Gamma$ and $U(z, P_\gamma) < U(z', P_\gamma)$ for other $\gamma \in \Gamma$.

Ambiguity in the ranking of treatment rules is a generic problem. To illustrate in a simple setting, suppose that there are two treatments, outcomes lie in the unit interval, and the welfare of a treatment is its outcome; thus, $T = \{a, b\}$, $u[y(t), t, \xi] = y(t)$, and $Y = [0, 1]$. Consider the treatment rules that assign all persons to $t = a$ or, contrariwise, all to $t = b$. In state of nature γ, these rules yield population welfare $E_\gamma[y(a)]$ and $E_\gamma[y(b)]$, respectively. For each person j in the study population and each treatment t, outcome $y_j(t)$ is observable if and only if $s_j = t$. This and the Law of Iterated Expectations imply that

$$E_\gamma[y(a)] = E(y \mid s = a)P(s = a)$$
$$+ \, E_\gamma[y(a) \mid s = b]P(s = b), \qquad (2.4\,a)$$
$$E_\gamma[y(b)] = E(y \mid s = b)P(s = b)$$
$$+ \, E_\gamma[y(b) \mid s = a]P(s = a). \qquad (2.4\,b)$$

The counterfactual quantities

$$\{E_\gamma[y(a) \mid s = b], E_\gamma[y(b) \mid s = a]\}$$

can take any value in the unit square. Suppose that

$$0 < E(y \mid s = a) < 1 \quad \text{and} \quad 0 < E(y \mid s = b) < 1.$$

Then inspection of (2.4) shows that

$$\{E_\gamma[y(a) \mid s = b] = 1, \ E_\gamma[y(b) \mid s = a] = 0\}$$
$$\Rightarrow E_\gamma[y(a)] > E_\gamma[y(b)],$$
$$\{E_\gamma[y(a) \mid s = b] = 0, \ E_\gamma[y(b) \mid s = a] = 1\}$$
$$\Rightarrow E_\gamma[y(a)] < E_\gamma[y(b)].$$

Hence, the ranking of these rules is ambiguous.

More generally, let

$$u_{0t\xi} \equiv \inf_{y \in Y} u(y, t, \xi) \quad \text{and} \quad u_{1t\xi} \equiv \sup_{y \in Y} u(y, t, \xi).$$

Let $z \in Z$ and $z' \in Z$ be any two feasible treatment rules. By (1.1), the difference in the population welfare delivered by these rules in state of nature γ is

$$U(z, P_\gamma) - U(z', P_\gamma)$$
$$= \sum_{\xi \in X} P(x = \xi) \sum_{t \in T} [z(t, \xi) - z'(t, \xi)] E_\gamma[u(t) \mid x = \xi].$$
$$(2.5)$$

The Law of Iterated Expectations and empirical knowledge of $P(x, s, y)$ give

$$E_\gamma[u(t) \mid x = \xi]$$
$$= E[u(t) \mid x = \xi, \ s = t] P(s = t \mid x = \xi)$$
$$+ E_\gamma[u(t) \mid x = \xi, \ s \neq t] P(s \neq t \mid x = \xi). \quad (2.6)$$

The counterfactual quantities

$$\{E_\gamma[u(t) \mid x = \xi, \ s \neq t], \ (t, \xi) \in T \times X\}$$

can take any value in the hyper-rectangle

$$\{[u_{0t\xi}, u_{1t\xi}], \ (t, \xi) \in T \times X\}.$$

Hence, the sharp lower bound on $U(z, P_\gamma) - U(z', P_\gamma)$ is obtained by setting these quantities at their lower bounds when $z(t, \xi) > z'(t, \xi)$ and at their upper bounds when $z(t, \xi) < z'(t, \xi)$. Thus,

$$\inf_{\gamma \in \Gamma} U(z, P_\gamma) - U(z', P_\gamma)$$
$$\equiv \sum_{\xi \in X} P(x = \xi) \sum_{t \in T} [z(t, \xi) - z'(t, \xi)]$$
$$\times [E\{u(t) \mid x = \xi, \ s = t\} P(s = t \mid x = \xi)$$
$$+ \{u_{1t\xi} \mathbf{1}[z(t, \xi) < z'(t,)]$$
$$+ u_{0t\xi} \mathbf{1}[z(t, \xi) > z'(t, \xi)]\}$$
$$\times P(s \neq t \mid x = \xi)], \quad (2.7)$$

where $\mathbf{1}[\cdot]$ is the indicator function taking the value 1 if the statement in brackets is true and 0 otherwise. Rule z dominates z' if the right-hand side of (2.7) is positive but not if the right-hand side is negative.

2.1.2 *Treatment Choice Under Ambiguity*

Ambiguity in the ranking of treatment rules means that a planner does not know which rule is optimal. However, ambiguity does not imply that a planner should be paralyzed, unwilling and unable to choose a rule. One could reasonably choose a rule that works well on average or one that works well uniformly over Γ. Bayes rules average across states of nature. The maximin- and minimax-regret criteria interpret in different ways the idea of uniformly good behavior. A maximin rule yields the greatest lower bound on population welfare across all states of nature. A minimax-regret rule yields the least upper bound on the loss in welfare that results from not knowing the state of nature.

Bayes Rules

Bayesian decision theorists recommend that a decision maker should place a subjective probability distribution on the states of nature and make a choice that works well on average, with respect to this subjective distribution. Thus, a Bayesian planner would place a subjective distribution π on Γ and solve the optimization problem

$$\sup_{z \in Z} \int U(z, P_\gamma) \, d\pi(\gamma). \tag{2.8}$$

The definition of $U(z, P_\gamma)$ and the Law of Iterated Expectations give

$$\int U(z, P_\gamma) \, d\pi(\gamma)$$
$$= \sum_{\xi \in X} P(x = \xi) \sum_{t \in T} z(t, \xi)$$
$$\times \{E[u(t) \mid x = \xi, \ s = t] P(s = t \mid x = \xi)$$
$$+ q(t, \xi) P(s \neq t \mid x = \xi)\}, \tag{2.9}$$

where

$$q(t, \xi) \equiv \int E_\gamma[u(t) \mid x = \xi, \ s \neq t] \, d\pi(\gamma)$$

is the planner's subjective mean for the counterfactual value of mean welfare under treatment t. Hence, the supremum in (2.8) is achieved if, for each $\xi \in X$, the planner chooses $z(\cdot, \xi)$ to solve the problem

$$\max_{z(\cdot, \xi) \in S} \sum_{t \in T} z(t, \xi)$$
$$\times \{E[u(t) \mid x = \xi, \ s = t] P(s = t \mid x = \xi)$$
$$+ q(t, \xi) P(s \neq t \mid x = \xi)\}, \tag{2.10}$$

where S is the unit simplex in $R^{|T|}$. The maximum in (2.10) is achieved by a singleton rule that allocates all persons with covariates ξ to a treatment solving the problem

$$\max_{t \in T} E[u(t) \mid x = \xi, \ s = t] P(s = t \mid x = \xi)$$
$$+ q(t, \xi) P(s \neq t \mid x = \xi). \quad (2.11)$$

Solution of problem (2.11) gives the Bayes rule, whatever Γ and π may be. Observe that π affects decision-making entirely through the subjective means $q(\cdot, \cdot)$. When Γ indexes the states of nature that are feasible given knowledge of $P(x, s, y)$, varying π can make $[q(t, \xi), \ (t, \xi) \in T \times X]$ take any value in the hyper-rectangle $\{[u_{0t\xi}, u_{1t\xi}], \ (t, \xi) \in T \times X\}$. In this way, the Bayes rule depends on the subjective distribution that the planner places on the feasible states of nature.

Bayesians often present *procedural rationality* arguments for use of Bayes rules. Savage (1954) showed that a decision maker whose choices are consistent with certain axioms can be interpreted as using a Bayes rule. Many decision theorists consider the Savage axioms appealing, but the axioms do not imply that chosen actions yield good outcomes. Berger (1985, p. 121) calls attention to this, stating: "A Bayesian analysis may be 'rational' in the weak axiomatic sense, yet be terrible in a practical sense if an inappropriate prior distribution is used."

Maximin Criterion

The idea of finding a rule that works well uniformly over Γ has mainly been interpreted in two ways. One is the *maximin* criterion:

$$\sup_{z \in Z} \inf_{\gamma \in \Gamma} U(z, P_\gamma). \quad (2.12)$$

When Γ indexes the states of nature that are feasible given knowledge of $P(x, s, y)$,

$$\inf_{\gamma \in \Gamma} U(z, P_\gamma)$$

$$= \inf_{\gamma \in \Gamma} \sum_{\xi \in X} P(x = \xi) \sum_{t \in T} z(t, \xi) E_\gamma[u(t) \mid x = \xi]$$

$$= \sum_{\xi \in X} P(x = \xi) \sum_{t \in T} z(t, \xi)$$

$$\times \{E[u(t) \mid x = \xi, \ s = t]P(s = t \mid x = \xi)$$

$$+ u_{0t\xi} P(s \neq t \mid x = \xi)\}.$$
$$(2.13)$$

Hence, a maximin rule allocates all persons with covariates ξ to a treatment that solves the problem

$$\max_{t \in T} E[u(t) \mid x = \xi, \ s = t]P(s = t \mid x = \xi)$$

$$+ u_{0t\xi} P(s \neq t \mid x = \xi). \quad (2.14)$$

The maximin criterion is simple to apply and to comprehend. From the maximin perspective, the desirability of treatment t increases with the mean welfare $E[u(t) \mid x = \xi, \ s = t]$ realized by persons in the study population who received the treatment and with the fraction $P(s = t \mid x = \xi)$ of persons who received the treatment. The second factor gives form to the conservatism of the maximin rule. All else equal, the more prevalent a treatment was in the study population, the more expedient it is to choose this treatment in the population of interest.

Minimax-Regret Criterion

The other main interpretation of uniformity is the minimax-regret criterion:

$$\inf_{z \in Z} \sup_{\gamma \in \Gamma} U^*(P_\gamma) - U(z, P_\gamma). \quad (2.15)$$

Here, $U^*(P_\gamma)$ is the optimal population mean welfare that would be achievable if it were known that $P = P_\gamma$; that is, by (1.5),

$$U^*(P_\gamma) \equiv \sum_{\xi \in X} P(x = \xi)$$

$$\times \left\{ \max_{t \in T} \int u[y(t), t, \xi] \, dP_\gamma[y(t) \mid x = \xi] \right\}.$$

$$(2.16)$$

The quantity $U^*(P_\gamma) - U(z, P_\gamma)$, called the *regret* of rule z in state of nature γ, is the loss in welfare that results from not knowing the true state of nature.

The minimax-regret criterion is generally more complex than maximin, but a relatively simple result emerges when there are two treatments. The following proposition gives the minimax-regret rule in this case.

Proposition 2.1. *Let* $T = \{a, b\}$. *Let* Γ *index the states of nature that are feasible given knowledge of* $P(x, s, y)$. *Let*

$$e_{t\xi} \equiv E[u(t) \mid x = \xi, \ s = t] \text{ and } p_{t\xi} \equiv P(s = t \mid x = \xi).$$

Then the minimax-regret rule is

$$z^{\mathrm{mr}}(b, \xi) = \begin{cases} 1 & \text{if } p_{a\xi}(e_{a\xi} - u_{0b\xi}) + p_{b\xi}(u_{1a\xi} - e_{b\xi}) < 0, \\[4pt] 0 & \text{if } p_{a\xi}(u_{1b\xi} - e_{a\xi}) + p_{b\xi}(e_{b\xi} - u_{0a\xi}) < 0, \\[4pt] \dfrac{p_{a\xi}(u_{1b\xi} - e_{a\xi}) + p_{b\xi}(e_{b\xi} - u_{0a\xi})}{p_{a\xi}(u_{1b\xi} - u_{0b\xi}) + p_{b\xi}(u_{1a\xi} - u_{0a\xi})} \\[4pt] & \text{otherwise.} \end{cases}$$

$$(2.17)$$

Proof. The Law of Iterated Expectations and knowledge of $P(x, s, y)$ give

$$E_\gamma[u(t) \mid x = \xi] = e_{t\xi}p_{t\xi} + E_\gamma[u(t) \mid x = \xi, \ s \neq t](1 - p_{t\xi}).$$

All quantities on the right-hand side are known except for

$$E_\gamma[u(t) \mid x = \xi, \ s \neq t],$$

which can take any value in the interval $[u_{0t\xi}, u_{1t\xi}]$. Hence, the regret of rule z in state of nature γ is

$$U^*(P_\gamma) - U(z, P_\gamma)$$

$$= \sum_{\xi \in X} P(x = \xi) \bigg\{ \max_{t \in T}[e_{t\xi}p_{t\xi} + \kappa_{\gamma t\xi}(1 - p_{t\xi})]$$

$$- \sum_{t \in T} z(t, \xi)[e_{t\xi}p_{t\xi} + \kappa_{\gamma t\xi}(1 - p_{t\xi})] \bigg\},$$

where $\kappa_{\gamma t\xi} \in [u_{0t\xi}, u_{1t\xi}]$ is a possible value of

$$E_\gamma[u(t) \mid x = \xi, \ s \neq t].$$

Maximum regret is

$$\sum_{\xi \in X} P(x = \xi)$$

$$\times \max_{(\kappa_{\gamma t\xi}, t \in T) \in \{[u_{0t\xi}, u_{1t\xi}], t \in T\}} \bigg\{ \max_{t \in T}[e_{t\xi}p_{t\xi} + \kappa_{\gamma t\xi}(1 - p_{t\xi})]$$

$$- \sum_{t \in T} z(t, \xi)[e_{t\xi}p_{t\xi} + \kappa_{\gamma t\xi}(1 - p_{t\xi})] \bigg\}.$$

Let $C(t, \xi)$ be the set of values of $(\kappa_{\gamma t\xi}, \ t \in T)$ such that treatment t is optimal for persons with covariates ξ; that is, $C(t, \xi) \equiv (\kappa_{\gamma t\xi}, \ t \in T)$ such that

$$e_{t\xi}p_{t\xi} + \kappa_{\gamma t\xi}(1 - p_{t\xi}) \geqslant e_{s\xi}p_{s\xi} + \kappa_{\gamma s\xi}(1 - p_{s\xi}), \quad s \in T.$$

Within this set, regret is maximized by setting

$$\kappa_{\gamma t\xi} = u_{1t\xi} \quad \text{and} \quad \kappa_{\gamma s\xi} = u_{0s\xi}, \quad s \neq t.$$

Thus,

$$\max_{(\kappa_{\gamma t\xi},t\in T)\in C(t,\xi)} \left\{ \max_{t\in T}[e_{t\xi}p_{t\xi} + \kappa_{\gamma t\xi}(1-p_{t\xi})] \right.$$
$$\left. - \sum_{t\in T} z(t,\xi)[e_{t\xi}p_{t\xi} + \kappa_{\gamma t\xi}(1-p_{t\xi})] \right\}$$
$$= [1 - z(t,\xi)][e_{t\xi}p_{t\xi} + u_{1t\xi}(1-p_{t\xi})]$$
$$- \sum_{s\neq t} z(s,\xi)[e_{s\xi}p_{s\xi} + u_{0s\xi}(1-p_{s\xi})].$$

Hence,

$$\max_{(\kappa_{\gamma t\xi},t\in T)\in\{[u_{0t\xi},u_{1t\xi}],t\in T\}} \left\{ \max_{t\in T}[e_{t\xi}p_{t\xi} + \kappa_{\gamma t\xi}(1-p_{t\xi})] \right.$$
$$\left. - \sum_{t\in T} z(t,\xi)[e_{t\xi}p_{t\xi} + \kappa_{\gamma t\xi}(1-p_{t\xi})] \right\}$$
$$= \max_{t\in T} \left\{ [1 - z(t,\xi)][e_{t\xi}p_{t\xi} + u_{1t\xi}(1-p_{t\xi})] \right.$$
$$\left. - \sum_{s\neq t} z(s,\xi)[e_{s\xi}p_{s\xi} + u_{0s\xi}(1-p_{s\xi})] \right\}.$$

It follows that, for each $\xi \in X$, the minimax-regret rule solves the problem

$$\min_{[z(t,\xi),t\in T]\in S^{|T|}}$$
$$\times \max_{t\in T} \left\{ [1 - z(t,\xi)][e_{t\xi}p_{t\xi} + u_{1t\xi}(1-p_{t\xi})] \right.$$
$$\left. - \sum_{s\neq t} z(s,\xi)[e_{s\xi}p_{s\xi} + u_{0s\xi}(1-p_{s\xi})] \right\}.$$

When there are two treatments, $t = a$ and $t = b$, the above simplifies to

$$\min_{\alpha \in [0,1]} \max\{(1 - \alpha)[e_{b\xi}p_{b\xi} + u_{1b\xi}p_{a\xi} - e_{a\xi}p_{a\xi} - u_{0a\xi}p_{b\xi}],$$

$$\alpha[e_{a\xi}p_{a\xi} + u_{1a\xi}p_{b\xi} - e_{b\xi}p_{b\xi} - u_{0b\xi}p_{a\xi}]\},$$

where $\alpha \equiv z(b, \xi)$ and where we use the fact that $p_{a\xi} + p_{b\xi} = 1$. The minimum occurs at $\alpha = 1$ if $e_{a\xi}p_{a\xi} + u_{1a\xi}p_{b\xi} - e_{b\xi}p_{b\xi} - u_{0b\xi}p_{a\xi} < 0$ and at $\alpha = 0$ if $e_{b\xi}p_{b\xi} + u_{1b\xi}p_{a\xi} - e_{a\xi}p_{a\xi} - u_{0a\xi}p_{b\xi} < 0$. If neither of these conditions occur, the minimum solves the equation

$$(1 - \alpha)[e_{b\xi}p_{b\xi} + u_{1b\xi}p_{a\xi} - e_{a\xi}p_{a\xi} - u_{0a\xi}p_{b\xi}]$$

$$= \alpha[e_{a\xi}p_{a\xi} + u_{1a\xi}p_{b\xi} - e_{b\xi}p_{b\xi} - u_{0b\xi}p_{a\xi}].$$

This yields

$$\alpha = \frac{p_{a\xi}(u_{1b\xi} - e_{a\xi}) + p_{b\xi}(e_{b\xi} - u_{0a\xi})}{p_{a\xi}(u_{1b\xi} - u_{0b\xi}) + p_{b\xi}(u_{1a\xi} - u_{0a\xi})}.$$

□

The proposition shows that the minimax-regret rule allocates all persons with covariates ξ to treatment b if that treatment dominates treatment a; this is the importance of the inequality $p_{a\xi}(e_{a\xi} - u_{0b\xi}) + p_{b\xi}(u_{1a\xi} - e_{b\xi}) < 0$. Similarly, the rule allocates all persons to treatment a if that treatment dominates b. When neither treatment dominates, the minimax-regret rule assigns positive fractions of observationally identical persons to both treatments. Indeed, nondominance is generic if $u_{0a\xi} = u_{0b\xi}$ and $u_{1a\xi} = u_{1b\xi}$. Intuitively, the fraction of persons allocated to treatment b increases with $e_{b\xi}$, which measures the observable success of treatment b, and decreases with $e_{a\xi}$, which measures the observable success of treatment a.

The fractional treatment allocations characteristic of the minimax-regret rule contrast sharply with those of the Bayes rules and the maximin rule, which generally assign all observationally identical persons to the same treatment. In some settings, legal requirements for "equal treatment of equals" may prevent planners from implementing the minimax-regret rule or other treatment rules that randomly allocate observationally identical persons across different treatments. However, such rules are entirely sensible from the utilitarian perspective. Proposition 2.1 gives a principled argument for diversification when making decisions under ambiguity.

2.1.3 Illustration: Sentencing and Recidivism of Juvenile Offenders

To illustrate treatment choice using the empirical evidence alone, consider a judge who must choose sentences for convicted juvenile offenders. Ample data are available on the outcomes experienced by offenders given the sentences that they actually receive. However, criminologists have long debated the counterfactual outcomes that offenders would experience if they were to receive other sentences. Moreover, the sentencing rules that judges have actually used are largely unknown (see Manski and Nagin 1998, Sections 2 and 4). Thus, sentencing is a treatment choice problem that might reasonably be studied using the empirical evidence alone.

Manski and Nagin (1998) analyzed data on the sentencing and recidivism of male offenders under the age of 16 living in the state of Utah. We compared recidivism under the two main sentencing options available to judges: confinement in residential facilities ($t = b$) and sentences that do not involve confinement ($t = a$). The outcome of interest was taken to be a binary measure of recidivism, with $y = 1$ if an offender is not convicted of a subsequent crime in the two-year period following sentencing, and $y = 0$ otherwise. The present discussion supposes that this binary outcome measures welfare; thus, $u[y(t), t, \xi] = y(t)$.

The distribution of treatments and outcomes in the study population was

$$P(s = b) = 0.11,$$
$$P(y = 1 \mid s = b) = 0.23,$$
$$P(y = 1 \mid s = a) = 0.41.$$

The resulting identification regions for $P[y(a) = 1]$ and $P[y(b) = 1]$ are the intervals $[0.36, 0.47]$ and $[0.03, 0.92]$, respectively. The problem is to use this empirical evidence to choose treatments for an analogous population of offenders who have not yet been sentenced.

The Bayes rule (2.11) depends on the subjective distribution that the planner places on the feasible states of nature. The Bayes rule assigns all offenders to treatment a if

$$P(y = 1 \mid s = a)P(s = a) + q(a)P(s = b)$$
$$> P(y = 1 \mid s = b)P(s = b) + q(b)P(s = a),$$

where

$$q(t) = \int P_\gamma[y(t) = 1 \mid s \neq t] \, d\pi(\gamma)$$

is the planner's subjective mean value for the counterfactual probability of no future criminality under treatment t. It assigns all to treatment b if the reverse inequality holds, and is indifferent among alternative assignments if the left- and right-hand side quantities are equal. Thus, the Bayes rule assigns all offenders to treatment a if $0.36 + 0.11q(a) > 0.03 + 0.89q(b)$ and all to treatment b if $0.36 + 0.11q(a) < 0.03 + 0.89q(b)$.

The maximin criterion (2.14) compares the worst feasible values of population welfare under the two treatments. In this illustration, the worst feasible welfare values are 0.36 and 0.03 for treatments a and b, respectively. Hence, $t = a$ is the maximin treatment.

Equation (2.17) gives the minimax-regret rule. In this illustration, $e_{b\xi} = 0.23$, $p_{b\xi} = 0.11$, $e_{a\xi} = 0.41$, $p_{a\xi} = 0.89$, and $\{u_{0t\xi} = 0,\ u_{1t\xi} = 1\}$, $t = a, b$. Hence, the minimax-regret rule assigns 0.55 of all offenders to treatment b and 0.45 to treatment a.

The above calculations suppose that male offenders under the age of 16 living in Utah are observationally identical. In fact, judges know the number of "prior referrals" of each offender; that is, the number of times an offender has previously been sentenced by the Utah juvenile justice system for commission of an offense. Treatment response may vary with the number of prior referrals. Hence, judges may want to condition treatment choice on this covariate.

Let x indicate whether an offender has 0, 1, or at least 2 prior referrals. The distribution of treatments and outcomes in the study population, conditional on x, was as follows:

$$P(s = b \mid x = 0) = 0.04,$$
$$P(y = 1 \mid x = 0,\ s = b) = 0.43,$$
$$P(y = 1 \mid x = 0,\ s = a) = 0.52,$$

$$P(s = b \mid x = 1) = 0.11,$$
$$P(y = 1 \mid x = 1,\ s = b) = 0.23,$$
$$P(y = 1 \mid x = 1,\ s = a) = 0.30,$$

$$P(s = b \mid x \geqslant 2) = 0.27,$$
$$P(y = 1 \mid x \geqslant 2,\ s = b) = 0.14,$$
$$P(y = 1 \mid x \geqslant 2,\ s = a) = 0.16.$$

Thus, offenders with high numbers of referrals were more likely to be sentenced to residential confinement and, conditional on their sentences, were more likely to commit future crimes.

For $\xi \in (0, 1, 2+)$, the Bayes rule assigns all offenders with ξ prior referrals to treatment a if

$$
\begin{aligned}
P(y = 1 \mid x = \xi, \ s = a)P(s = a \mid x = \xi) \\
+ q(a, \xi)P(s = b \mid x = \xi) \\
> P(y = 1 \mid x = \xi, \ s = b)P(s = b \mid x = \xi) \\
+ q(b, \xi)P(s = a \mid x = \xi),
\end{aligned}
$$

and all to treatment b if the reverse inequality holds. The maximin rule is $s = a$ for all values of x. The minimax-regret treatment allocations are $z^{\mathrm{mr}}(b, 0) = 0.48$, $z^{\mathrm{mr}}(b, 1) = 0.65$, and $z^{\mathrm{mr}}(b, 2+) = 0.65$.

2.1.4 *Treatment Choice Using Assumptions about Counterfactual Outcomes*

Thus far, this section has shown that a planner who only observes the outcomes experienced by the study population may nevertheless apply reasonable, even if not demonstrably optimal criteria to choose treatments. What of a planner who is willing to maintain assumptions about the counterfactual outcomes not experienced by the study population? Then the set Γ of feasible states of nature should reflect these assumptions as well as the planner's empirical knowledge of $P(x, s, y)$. This done, equations (2.8), (2.12), and (2.15) still give the Bayesian, maximin, and minimax-regret prescriptions for treatment choice.

The longstanding tradition in research on treatment response has been to impose assumptions strong enough to make Γ a singleton when combined with knowledge of $P(x, s, y)$. It has been particularly common to assume that, among persons in the study population who share the same covariates, persons who received different status quo treatments have the same distribution of treatment response; that is,

$$P[y(\cdot) \mid x, s] = P[y(\cdot) \mid x]. \qquad (2.18)$$

This assumption, which is most credible when members of the study population are randomly assigned to treatments, implies that $P[y(t) \mid x = \xi] = P(y \mid x = \xi, s = t)$, $(t, \xi) \in T \times X$. Hence, the treatment response distributions $P[y(t) \mid x = \xi]$, $(t, \xi) \in T \times X$ are point identified.

Given (2.18) or another assumption that makes Γ a singleton, the Bayesian, maximin, and minimax-regret prescriptions for treatment choice all reduce to

$$\sup_{z \in Z} U(z, P_\gamma),$$

where γ is the sole member of Γ. Solving this optimization problem delivers the optimal treatment rule if the maintained assumptions are correct, in which case $P_\gamma = P$. However, a rule solving $\sup_{z \in Z} U(z, P_\gamma)$ need not be optimal if $P_\gamma \neq P$. This is important because assumptions that are strong enough to make Γ a singleton may carry little credibility.

A planner who lacks confidence in assumptions that make Γ a singleton may reasonably want to choose treatments using weaker but more credible assumptions. A multitude of such assumptions may warrant consideration, and it is impossible here to provide an exhaustive analysis of their implications. To give a sense of the possibilities, Section 2.2 studies treatment choice when response is assumed to vary monotonically with a real-valued treatment. Section 2.3 considers *exclusion restrictions* that assert equality of outcome distributions across persons with different covariates.

2.2   Monotone Treatment Response

In many planning problems t measures the magnitude of a resource, such as money or time, that a planner can invest in treatment of a person and $y_j(t)$ is the return to this investment, with treatments and outcomes measured in the same units. It is often reasonable to assume that increasing the amount invested does not decrease the outcome achieved. This section considers treatment choice in such scenarios.

Formally, let the treatment set T and outcome space Y be bounded subsets of the real line. Let welfare equal the outcome minus the magnitude of the treatment; that is, $u[y(t), t, x] = y(t) - t$. The assumption of monotone treatment response (MTR) posits that, for each person j, $y_j(\cdot)$ is a weakly increasing function on T. This assumption does not require that everyone has the same treatment response function; outcomes may increase strongly with treatment for some people and weakly or not at all for others. The identifying power of the MTR assumption has been studied in Manski (1997), on which this section builds.

Combining the MTR assumption with observation of the treatments and outcomes experienced by the study population yields information about their counterfactual outcomes. Let $y_0 \equiv \inf Y$ and $y_1 \equiv \sup Y$. For each person j in the study population, monotonicity of $y_j(\cdot)$ and observation of (s_j, y_j) reveals that $y_j(\cdot)$ is a monotone function that takes values in the range $[y_0, y_1]$ and that passes through the point $(s_j, y(s_j))$. In particular, we learn the following about outcomes under counterfactual treatments:

$$\left.\begin{aligned} t < s_j &\Rightarrow y_0 \leqslant y_j(t) \leqslant y_j, \\ t > s_j &\Rightarrow y_j \leqslant y_j(t) \leqslant y_1. \end{aligned}\right\} \qquad (2.19)$$

Thus, the observed outcome y_j is an upper (lower) bound on $y_j(t)$ when the counterfactual treatment t is smaller (larger) than s_j.

To see how the MTR assumption helps to identify mean treatment response, let $(t, \xi) \in T \times X$ and use the Law of Iterated Expectations to write

$$
\begin{aligned}
E_\gamma[y(t) \mid x = \xi] \\
= E(y \mid x = \xi, \ s = t) P(s = t \mid x = \xi) \\
+ \sum_{k<t} E_\gamma[y(t) \mid x = \xi, \ s = k] P(s = k \mid x = \xi) \\
+ \sum_{k>t} E_\gamma[y(t) \mid x = \xi, \ s = k] P(s = k \mid x = \xi).
\end{aligned}
$$

$$(2.20)$$

The MTR assumption implies that, for each $k \in T$,

$$
\begin{aligned}
t' > t \ \Rightarrow \ E_\gamma[y(t') \mid x = \xi, \ s = k] \\
\geqslant E_\gamma[y(t) \mid x = \xi, \ s = k]. \quad (2.21)
\end{aligned}
$$

Empirical knowledge of $P(x, s, y)$ informs the planner that $E[y(k) \mid x = \xi, \ s = k] = E(y \mid x = \xi, \ s = k)$. Hence, combining the MTR assumption with the empirical evidence yields these restrictions on the counterfactual quantities in (2.20):

$$
\left.
\begin{aligned}
k < t \ \Rightarrow \ E_\gamma[y(t) \mid x = \xi, \ s = k] \\
\in [E(y \mid x = \xi, \ s = k), y_1], \\
k > t \ \Rightarrow \ E_\gamma[y(t) \mid x = \xi, \ s = k] \\
\in [y_0, E(y \mid x = \xi, \ s = k)].
\end{aligned}
\right\} \quad (2.22)
$$

There are no restrictions across covariate values. Hence, (2.21) and (2.22) completely describe what the MTR assumption and empirical knowledge of $P(x, s, y)$ together reveal about the counterfactual determinants of mean treatment response.

With this as background, now consider the Bayes, maximin, and minimax-regret criteria.

Bayes Rules

As in Section 2.1, problem (2.11) yields the Bayes rule. What differs is that the subjective means $[q(t, \xi), (t, \xi) \in T \times X]$ can now take values only in a subset of the hyper-rectangle $\{[u_{0t\xi}, u_{1t\xi}], (t, \xi) \in T \times X\}$. For each value of (t, ξ),

$$q(t, \xi) = \sum_{k \neq t} \left\{ \int E_\gamma[y(t) \mid x = \xi, \ s = k] \, d\pi(\gamma) \right\}$$
$$\times P(s = k \mid x = \xi). \quad (2.23)$$

Equation (2.22) implies that the feasible values for $q(t, \xi)$ are as follows:

$$q(t, \xi) \in [E(y \mid x = \xi, \ s < t)P(s < t \mid x = \xi)$$
$$+ y_0 P(s > t \mid x = \xi),$$
$$y_1 P(s < t \mid x = \xi)$$
$$+ E(y \mid x = \xi, \ s > t)P(s > t \mid x = \xi)].$$
$$(2.24)$$

Moreover, (2.21) implies that $t' > t \Rightarrow q(t', \xi) \geqslant q(t, \xi)$.

Maximin Criterion

Let Γ_{MTR} index the states of nature that are feasible given the MTR assumption and empirical knowledge of $P(x, s, y)$. For each treatment rule z,

$$\inf_{\gamma \in \Gamma_{\mathrm{MTR}}} U(z, P_\gamma) = \inf_{\gamma \in \Gamma_{\mathrm{MTR}}} \sum_{\xi \in X} P(x = \xi)$$
$$\times \sum_{t \in T} z(t, \xi)\{E_\gamma[y(t) \mid x = \xi] - t\}.$$
$$(2.25)$$

The maximin criterion maximizes this expression over all feasible treatment rules.

The extremum problem (2.25) is solved by the state of nature in which every member of the study population has his smallest feasible response function; that is, $y_j(t) = y_0$ for $t < s_j$ and $y_j(t) = y_j$ for $t \geqslant s_j$. This state of nature jointly minimizes $\{E_\gamma[y(t) \mid x = \xi], \ (t, \xi) \in T \times X\}$. In particular,

$$\inf_{\gamma \in \Gamma_{\mathrm{MTR}}} E_\gamma[y(t) \mid x = \xi]$$
$$= y_0 P(s > t \mid x = \xi)$$
$$+ E(y \mid x = \xi, \ s \leqslant t) P(s \leqslant t \mid x = \xi).$$
$$(2.26)$$

It follows that the maximin rule allocates all persons with covariates ξ to a treatment that solves the problem

$$\max_{t \in T} y_0 P(s > t \mid x = \xi)$$
$$+ E(y \mid x = \xi, \ s \leqslant t) P(s \leqslant t \mid x = \xi) - t. \quad (2.27)$$

Minimax-Regret Criterion

By definition, the minimax-regret criterion is

$$\inf_{z \in Z} \sup_{\gamma \in \Gamma_{\mathrm{MTR}}} \sum_{\xi \in X} P(x = \xi)$$
$$\times \left\{ \max_{t \in T} \{ E_\gamma[y(t) \mid x = \xi] - t \} \right.$$
$$\left. - \sum_{t \in T} z(t, \xi) \{ E_\gamma[y(t) \mid x = \xi] - t \} \right\}.$$
$$(2.28)$$

In general, the minimax-regret rule does not have a simple form like the maximin or Bayes rules. However, a simple result does emerge when there are two treatments. Without loss of generality, let these be $t = 0$ and 1. The following proposition derives the minimax-regret rule in this case.

Proposition 2.2. *Let* $T = \{0, 1\}$. *Let* Γ_{MTR} *index the states of nature that are feasible given the MTR assumption and empirical knowledge of* $P(x, s, y)$. *Let* $e_{t\xi} \equiv E(y \mid x = \xi, \ s = t)$ *and* $p_{t\xi} \equiv P(s = t \mid x = \xi)$. *Then the minimax-regret rule is*

$$z^{\text{mr}}(1, \xi)$$

$$= \begin{cases} 0 & \text{if } e_{1\xi}p_{1\xi} + y_1p_{0\xi} - 1 - e_{0\xi}p_{0\xi} - y_0p_{1\xi} < 0, \\[2mm] \dfrac{e_{1\xi}p_{1\xi} + y_1p_{0\xi} - 1 - e_{0\xi}p_{0\xi} - y_0p_{1\xi}}{e_{1\xi}p_{1\xi} + y_1p_{0\xi} - e_{0\xi}p_{0\xi} - y_0p_{1\xi}} \\ & \text{otherwise.} \end{cases}$$

$$(2.29)$$

Proof. The regret of rule z in state of nature γ is

$$U^*(P_\gamma) - U(z, P_\gamma)$$

$$= \sum_{\xi \in X} P(x = \xi) \bigg\{ \max_{t \in T}[e_{t\xi}p_{t\xi} + \kappa_{\gamma t\xi}(1 - p_{t\xi}) - t]$$

$$- \sum_{t \in T} z(t, \xi)[e_{t\xi}p_{t\xi} + \kappa_{\gamma t\xi}(1 - p_{t\xi}) - t] \bigg\},$$

where $\kappa_{\gamma t\xi}$ is a possible value of $E[y(t) \mid x = \xi, \ s \neq t]$. Maximum regret is

$$\sum_{\xi \in X} P(x = \xi)$$

$$\times \max_{(\kappa_{\gamma 0\xi}, \kappa_{\gamma 1\xi}), \gamma \in \Gamma_{\text{MTR}}} \bigg\{ \max_{t \in T}[e_{t\xi}p_{t\xi} + \kappa_{\gamma t\xi}(1 - p_{t\xi}) - t]$$

$$- \sum_{t \in T} z(t, \xi)[e_{t\xi}p_{t\xi} + \kappa_{\gamma t\xi}(1 - p_{t\xi}) - t] \bigg\}.$$

Let $C(0, \xi)$ be the values of $(\kappa_{\gamma 0\xi}, \kappa_{\gamma 1\xi})$ such that treatment 0 is optimal for persons with covariates ξ; that is,

$$C(0, \xi) \equiv (\kappa_{\gamma 0\xi}, \kappa_{\gamma 1\xi})$$

such that

$$e_{0\xi} p_{0\xi} + \kappa_{\gamma 0\xi}(1 - p_{0\xi}) \geqslant e_{1\xi} p_{1\xi} + \kappa_{\gamma 1\xi}(1 - p_{1\xi}) - 1.$$

Within $C(0, \xi)$, regret is maximized by setting $\kappa_{\gamma 0\xi}$ at its upper bound given in (2.22) and $\kappa_{\gamma 1\xi}$ at its lower bound; that is, by setting $\kappa_{\gamma 0\xi} = e_{1\xi}$ and $\kappa_{\gamma 1\xi} = e_{0\xi}$. Thus,

$$
\max_{(\kappa_{\gamma 0\xi}, \kappa_{\gamma 1\xi}) \in C(0, \xi)} \left\{ \max_{t \in T}[e_{t\xi} p_{t\xi} + \kappa_{\gamma t\xi}(1 - p_{t\xi}) - t] \right.
$$

$$
\left. - \sum_{t \in T} z(t, \xi)[e_{t\xi} p_{t\xi} + \kappa_{\gamma t\xi}(1 - p_{t\xi}) - t] \right\}
$$

$$
= \alpha[e_{0\xi} p_{0\xi} + e_{1\xi}(1 - p_{0\xi})]
$$

$$
- \alpha[e_{1\xi} p_{1\xi} + e_{0\xi}(1 - p_{1\xi}) - 1]
$$

$$
= \alpha,
$$

where $\alpha \equiv z(1, \xi)$. Similarly, let $C(1, \xi)$ be the values of $(\kappa_{\gamma 0\xi}, \kappa_{\gamma 1\xi})$ such that treatment 1 is optimal for persons with covariates ξ. Within $C(1, \xi)$, regret is maximized by setting $\kappa_{\gamma 0\xi} = y_0$ and $\kappa_{\gamma 1\xi} = y_1$. Thus,

$$
\max_{(\kappa_{\gamma 0\xi}, \kappa_{\gamma 1\xi}) \in C(1, \xi)} \left\{ \max_{t \in T}[e_{t\xi} p_{t\xi} + \kappa_{\gamma t\xi}(1 - p_{t\xi}) - t] \right.
$$

$$
\left. - \sum_{t \in T} z(t, \xi)[e_{t\xi} p_{t\xi} + \kappa_{\gamma t\xi}(1 - p_{t\xi}) - t] \right\}
$$

$$
= (1 - \alpha)[e_{1\xi} p_{1\xi} + y_1(1 - p_{1\xi}) - 1]
$$

$$
- (1 - \alpha)[e_{0\xi} p_{0\xi} + y_0(1 - p_{0\xi})]
$$

$$
= (1 - \alpha)(e_{1\xi} p_{1\xi} + y_1 p_{0\xi} - 1 - e_{0\xi} p_{0\xi} - y_0 p_{1\xi}).
$$

Hence, for each $\xi \in X$, the minimax-regret rule solves the problem

$$\min_{[z(0,\xi),z(1,\xi)]\in S^2}$$

$$\max_{(\kappa_{\gamma 0 \xi},\kappa_{\gamma 1 \xi}),\gamma \in \Gamma_{\text{MTR}}} \left\{ \max_{t \in T}[e_{t\xi}p_{t\xi} + \kappa_{\gamma t\xi}(1 - p_{t\xi})] \right.$$

$$\left. - \sum_{t \in T} z(t,\xi)[e_{t\xi}p_{t\xi} + \kappa_{\gamma t\xi}(1 - p_{t\xi})] \right\}$$

$$= \min_{\alpha \in [0,1]} \max[\alpha, (1 - \alpha) \\ \times (e_{1\xi}p_{1\xi} + y_1 p_{0\xi} - 1 - e_{0\xi}p_{0\xi} - y_0 p_{1\xi})].$$

The minimum occurs at $\alpha = 0$ if

$$e_{1\xi}p_{1\xi} + y_1 p_{0\xi} - 1 - e_{0\xi}p_{0\xi} - y_0 p_{1\xi} < 0.$$

Otherwise, the minimum solves the equation

$$\alpha = (1 - \alpha)(e_{1\xi}p_{1\xi} + y_1 p_{0\xi} - 1 - e_{0\xi}p_{0\xi} - y_0 p_{1\xi}).$$

This yields

$$\alpha = \frac{e_{1\xi}p_{1\xi} + y_1 p_{0\xi} - 1 - e_{0\xi}p_{0\xi} - y_0 p_{1\xi}}{e_{1\xi}p_{1\xi} + y_1 p_{0\xi} - e_{0\xi}p_{0\xi} - y_0 p_{1\xi}}.$$

$$\square$$

The proposition shows that, when there is no dominant treatment, the minimax-regret rule assigns positive fractions of observationally identical persons to both treatments, the fraction allocated to treatment 1 increasing with $e_{1\xi}$ and decreasing with $e_{0\xi}$. The rule allocates all persons with covariates ξ to treatment 0 if that treatment dominates treatment 1; this occurs if

$$e_{1\xi}p_{1\xi} + y_1 p_{0\xi} - 1 - e_{0\xi}p_{0\xi} - y_0 p_{1\xi} < 0.$$

The rule never allocates all persons to treatment 1 because, under the MTR assumption, that treatment cannot dominate treatment 0. An easy way to see that treatment 1 cannot dominate 0 is to observe that a flat response function is feasible under the MTR assumption. If the response function is flat, treatment 1 yields lower welfare than treatment 0 because it delivers the same outcome but is more costly.

2.2.1 Illustration: Policing and Crime

Economists studying optimal law enforcement have commonly assumed that planners know how policing and sanctions affect offense rates (see Polinsky and Shavell 2000). However, empirical social scientists have found it difficult to acquire this knowledge. For example, Blumstein, Cohen, and Nagin (1978) explain why it has been so hard to establish the deterrent effect of capital punishment on murder. The National Research Council (2001) summarizes the very limited information available on the effectiveness of policing and sanctions in deterring drug supply and use.

In some settings, a planner may realistically have partial knowledge of the deterrent effect of law enforcement. In particular, a planner may observe offense rates in a study population and find it credible to assume that enforcement weakly deters crime; that is, offense behavior weakly decreases as enforcement increases. In such settings, the analysis of this section is applicable.

To illustrate treatment choice with the MTR assumption, let the population be selected cities in a state, province, or other governmental planning unit. Let the treatment be the expenditure per capita on policing in a city. Let the outcome be the monetized loss per capita that society suffers from crime, which I take to be proportional to the crime rate per capita. Then welfare is $\beta g(t) - t$, where t is police expenditure per capita, $g(t)$ is the crime rate per capita when police expenditure is t, and $\beta < 0$ is the monetized social loss per crime. It is reasonable to conjecture that a city's crime rate falls as its police expenditure rises; hence, $\beta g(t)$ rises with t. This is the assumption of monotone treatment response.

Suppose that the planner can observe past treatments and outcomes for cities in the relevant planning unit. I make no assumptions about the manner in which treatments were chosen in the past. For example, each city may have chosen its own police expenditures by weighing political, fiscal, and law enforcement considerations. Whatever the status quo treatment rule may have been, suppose that new legislation directs the planner to choose future treatment values. For simplicity, suppose that the legislation requires all cities to receive the same police expenditure per capita. Thus, the planner is not permitted to treat different cities differentially.

To illustrate empirically, I take the planning unit to be the state of Wisconsin and the population to be cities of moderate size, specifically those with population between 25 000 and 100 000. The US Bureau of the Census *County and City Data Book 2000* provides roughly contemporaneous data on annual police expenditure and crime rate per capita for each of the 21 such cities in Wisconsin. As shown in Table 2.1, annual police expenditure per capita ranged from a low of \$115 in Oshkosh to a high of \$260 in Racine. The annual crime rate per capita ranged from a low of 0.0157 in New Berlin to a high of 0.0629 in Racine.

I take the feasible treatments to be the set

$$T = [100, 120, \ldots, 280]$$

of values for spending per capita that span the realized treatment values in increments of \$20. Computation of treatment rules requires specification of lower and upper bounds on the crime rate per capita, as well as a value

Table 2.1. Policing and crime in Wisconsin.

	City	Police expenditure per capita ($)	Crimes per capita
1	Appleton	129	0.0260
2	Beloit	202	0.0473
3	Brookfield	143	0.0307
4	Eau Claire	130	0.0407
5	Fond du Lac	132	0.0395
6	Green Bay	164	0.0428
7	Greenfield	161	0.0388
8	Janesville	118	0.0549
9	Kenosha	157	0.0348
10	La Crosse	150	0.0412
11	Manitowoc	126	0.0424
12	Menomonee Falls	164	0.0193
13	New Berlin	146	0.0157
14	Oshkosh	115	0.0358
15	Racine	260	0.0629
16	Sheboygan	143	0.0426
17	Superior	163	0.0599
18	Waukesha	142	0.0233
19	Wausau	139	0.0380
20	Wauwatosa	200	0.0475
21	West Allis	205	0.0453

Source: US Bureau of the Census, *County and City Data Book 2000*, retrieved from the University of Virginia, Geospatial and Statistical Data Center: http://fisher.lib.virginia.edu/collections/stats/ccdb/. For each city, expenditures on police are for fiscal year 1996–1997 and number of serious crimes known to police are for 1999. Per capita figures are obtained by dividing by city population in July 1997.

for the parameter β. The logical lower bound on the crime rate is $g_0 = 0$; hence, $y_1 = \beta g_0 = 0$. There is no logical upper bound on the crime rate, so I consider

Table 2.2. Maximin- and minimax-regret treatment allocations. T, treatment; M, maximin; MR, minimax-regret; A, $g_1 = 0.1$, $\beta = -1000$; B, $g_1 = 0.2$; $\beta = -1000$; C, $g_1 = 0.1$, $\beta = -10\,000$; D, $g_1 = 0.2$, $\beta = -10\,000$.

T	A		B		C		D	
	M	MR	M	MR	M	MR	M	MR
100	1	0.31	0	0.12	0	0.03	0	0.01
120	0	0.25	0	0.12	0	0.03	0	0.01
140	0	0.24	0	0.14	0	0.02	0	0.01
160	0	0.20	0	0.19	0	0.03	0	0.02
180	0	0	1	0.34	0	0.05	0	0.03
200	0	0	0	0.09	0	0.02	0	0.02
220	0	0	0	0	1	0.05	0	0.05
240	0	0	0	0	0	0.05	0	0.05
260	0	0	0	0	0	0.03	0	0.03
280	0	0	0	0	0	0.69	1	0.76

two scenarios, one assuming that the crime rate at any feasible treatment value cannot exceed $g_1 = 0.1$ annual crimes per capita and the other assuming that it cannot exceed $g_1 = 0.2$ annual crimes per capita; in either case, $y_0 = \beta g_1$. The parameter β, which measures the monetized social loss per crime, should be chosen by the planner. I compute treatment rules in two scenarios, one setting $\beta = -\$1000$ and the other setting $\beta = -\$10\,000$.

Table 2.2 reports the maximin- and minimax-regret treatment rules in the four scenarios. It is intuitive that the chosen expenditure on policing should increase with g_1 and β. The maximin- and minimax-regret rules share this feature, but in strikingly different ways. Whereas the maximin rule always yields a singleton allocation, the minimax-regret rule yields a fractional allocation in all four scenarios.

2.2.2   Semi-Monotone Response

A natural extension of the planning problem considered in this section is to let t be a vector measuring the magnitudes of several resources that a planner can invest in treatment and let welfare be the outcome of treatment minus its cost. Thus, let T now be a bounded subset of a finite-dimensional real space and let welfare have the form $u[y(t), t, x] = y(t) - ct$, where c is a vector of resource prices.

The natural extension of the MTR assumption is to assume that treatment response is semi-monotone. Semi-monotonicity means monotonicity over all ordered pairs of treatments. A pair (t, t') of treatments is ordered, with $t \geqslant t'$, if all components of the vector t are at least as large as the corresponding components of t'. Thus, the assumption of semi-monotone response means that $y_j(t) \geqslant y_j(t')$ when $t \geqslant t'$. Semi-monotonicity places no restriction on the ordering of $y_j(t)$ and $y_j(t')$ when t and t' are unordered. In what follows, the notation $t \oslash t'$ indicates that a pair (t, t') is not ordered.

Whereas equation (2.19) expressed the implications of the MTR assumption for outcomes under counterfactual treatments, equation (2.30) does the same for the assumption of semi-monotone response:

$$\left. \begin{array}{l} t < s_j \;\Rightarrow\; y_0 \leqslant y_j(t) \leqslant y_j, \\ t > s_j \;\Rightarrow\; y_j \leqslant y_j(t) \leqslant y_1, \\ t \oslash s_j \;\Rightarrow\; y_0 \leqslant y_j(t) \leqslant y_1. \end{array} \right\} \qquad (2.30)$$

The first two parts of (2.30) correspond to (2.19). The new third part covers cases where treatments t and s_j are unordered.

Application of the maximin- and minimax-regret criteria with semi-monotonicity yields results that extend those reported above in obvious ways. For example, a maximin rule allocates all persons with covariates ξ to a treatment that solves the problem

$$\max_{t \in T} y_0 P(s > t \cup s \varnothing t \mid x = \xi)$$
$$+ E(y \mid x = \xi, \ s \leqslant t) P(s \leqslant t \mid x = \xi) - ct. \quad (2.31)$$

2.2.3 Concave Monotonicity

Monotonicity and semi-monotonicity are leading examples of assumptions that nonparametrically restrict the shape of response functions. Manski (1997) also studied identification when response functions are assumed to be both concave and monotone. This combination of assumptions is common in economic production analysis, where it is often assumed that increasing a factor of production has *diminishing marginal returns*. Combining concavity and monotonicity has substantially more identifying power than each assumption alone; informative bounds on mean treatment response emerge even when the outcome space Y is unbounded. However, the implications for treatment choice are more complex to study than those of monotonicity alone.

2.3 Exclusion Restrictions

Economists analyzing treatment response have long exploited assumptions that link the outcomes of persons with different observable covariates. Especially common has been the use of *exclusion restrictions* asserting equality of outcome distributions or mean outcomes across persons with different covariates. Exclusion restrictions combined with assumptions asserting homogeneity of treatment response yield point identification of response distributions (Heckman 1978; Heckman and Robb 1985). The identifying power of exclusion restrictions alone, not

combined with other assumptions, has been studied in
Manski (1990, 2003), on which this section builds.

Let the covariate space X have the product form $X =
W \times V$, and let the random variable x correspondingly
have the form $x = (w, v)$. A strong form of exclusion
restriction asserts that the response functions $y(\cdot)$ are
statistically independent of v, conditional on w; that is,

$$P[y(\cdot) \mid x] = P[y(\cdot) \mid w]. \qquad (2.32)$$

A weaker assumption asserts equality across v of the outcome distribution for each treatment:

$$P[y(t) \mid x] = P[y(t) \mid w], \quad t \in T. \qquad (2.33)$$

A still weaker assumption only asserts equality across v
of the mean welfare produced by each treatment:

$$E[u(t) \mid x] = E[u(t) \mid w], \quad t \in T. \qquad (2.34)$$

To see that assumption (2.33) implies (2.34), recall that
$u(t)$ is shorthand for $u(y, t, x)$.

In all of these cases, covariate v is termed an *instrumental variable*. Assumptions (2.32)–(2.34) are called
exclusion restrictions because, in one sense or another,
they exclude the possibility of association between outcomes and v.

I shall focus on assumption (2.34), which is the eas-
iest to study. To see how the assumption restricts the
feasible values for counterfactual outcomes in the study
population, let $\omega \in W$ and let $X_\omega \equiv \{\omega\} \times V$ be
the subset of X with $w = \omega$. As in Section 2.1, let
$e_{t\xi} \equiv E[u(t) \mid x = \xi, \ s = t]$, $p_{t\xi} \equiv P(s = t \mid x = \xi)$, and
$\kappa_{\gamma t \xi} = E_\gamma[u(t) \mid x = \xi, \ s \neq t]$. Now let ξ' and ξ'' be any
distinct elements of X_ω. The Law of Iterated Expecta-
tions and assumption (2.34) imply that, in feasible states

of nature,

$$E_\gamma[u(t) \mid x = \xi''] = e_{t\xi''}p_{t\xi''} + \kappa_{\gamma t\xi''}(1 - p_{t\xi''})$$
$$= e_{t\xi'}p_{t\xi'} + \kappa_{\gamma t\xi'}(1 - p_{t\xi'})$$
$$= E_\gamma[u(t) \mid x = \xi']. \qquad (2.35)$$

Thus, the counterfactual values $(\kappa_{\gamma t\xi}, \ \xi \in X_\omega)$ are jointly feasible if and only if they lie in the hyper-rectangle $\{[u_{0t\xi}, u_{1t\xi}], \ \xi \in X_\omega\}$ and satisfy the system of linear equations (2.35).

One may find that no values of $(\kappa_{\gamma t\xi}, \ \xi \in X_\omega)$ are feasible. If so, one should conclude that the asserted exclusion restriction is incorrect. The discussion below presumes that the restriction is correct and, hence, that feasible values of the counterfactuals do exist.

Now consider the Bayes, maximin-, and minimax-regret criteria. As in Section 2.1, problem (2.11) yields the Bayes rule. What differs is that, for each $t \in T$ and $\omega \in W$, the subjective means $[q(t, \xi), \ \xi \in X_\omega]$ must satisfy the linear equations

$$e_{t\xi''}p_{t\xi''} + q(t, \xi'')(1 - p_{t\xi''})$$
$$= e_{t\xi'}p_{t\xi'} + q(t, \xi')(1 - p_{t\xi'})$$
$$\text{for all } (\xi', \xi'') \in X_\omega \times X_\omega. \quad (2.36)$$

To compute a maximin rule, let z be any treatment rule and let ν be any element of V. It follows from (2.35) that the expected welfare of rule z in state of nature γ is

$$U(z, P_\gamma)$$
$$\equiv \sum_{\omega \in W} P(w = \omega)$$
$$\times \sum_{t \in T} z(t, \omega)[e_{t(\omega,\nu)}p_{t(\omega,\nu)} + \kappa_{\gamma t(\omega,\nu)}(1 - p_{t(\omega,\nu)})],$$
$$(2.37)$$

where

$$z(t, \omega) \equiv \sum_{\xi \in X_\omega} z(t, \xi) P(x = \xi \mid w = \omega).$$

Hence, a maximin rule allocates all persons with covariates ω to a treatment that solves the problem

$$\max_{t \in T}[e_{t(\omega,\nu)} p_{t(\omega,\nu)} + \lambda_{0t(\omega,\nu)}(1 - p_{t(\omega,\nu)})], \qquad (2.38)$$

where $\lambda_{0t(\omega,\nu)}$ is the smallest value of $\kappa_{\gamma t(\omega,\nu)}$ that is feasible given assumption (2.34).

The minimax-regret criterion is generally more complex but, as in Section 2.1, a simple result emerges when there are two treatments. Repeat the argument proving Proposition 2.1, using (2.37) to express expected welfare. Let $\lambda_{1t(\omega,\nu)}$ be the largest value of $\kappa_{\gamma t(\omega,\nu)}$ that is feasible given assumption (2.34). The result is the following proposition.

Proposition 2.3. *Let* $T = \{a, b\}$. *Let* Γ *index the feasible states of nature given knowledge of* $P(x, s, y)$ *and assumption (2.34). Then the minimax-regret rule is*

$$z^{\mathrm{mr}}(b, \omega) = \begin{cases} 1 & \text{if } p_{a(\omega,\nu)}(e_{a(\omega,\nu)} - \lambda_{0b(\omega,\nu)}) \\ & \quad + p_{b(\omega,\nu)}(\lambda_{1a(\omega,\nu)} - e_{b(\omega,\nu)}) < 0, \\ 0 & \text{if } p_{a(\omega,\nu)}(\lambda_{1b(\omega,\nu)} - e_{a(\omega,\nu)}) \\ & \quad + p_{b(\omega,\nu)}(e_{b(\omega,\nu)} - \lambda_{0a(\omega,\nu)}) < 0, \\ \dfrac{\begin{aligned}&p_{a(\omega,\nu)}(\lambda_{1b(\omega,\nu)} - e_{a(\omega,\nu)}) \\ &\quad + p_{b(\omega,\nu)}(e_{b(\omega,\nu)} - \lambda_{0a(\omega,\nu)})\end{aligned}}{\begin{aligned}&p_{a(\omega,\nu)}(\lambda_{1b(\omega,\nu)} - \lambda_{0b(\omega,\nu)}) \\ &\quad + p_{b(\omega,\nu)}(\lambda_{1a(\omega,\nu)} - \lambda_{0a(\omega,\nu)})\end{aligned}} \\ \quad \text{otherwise.} \end{cases}$$

$$(2.39)$$

2.3.1   Illustration: Sentencing and Recidivism of Juvenile Offenders

The empirical illustration of Section 2.1 considered how a judge may sentence juvenile offenders using the empirical evidence alone. A judge may conjecture that future criminality does not vary with the number of prior referrals, in the sense of (2.34). That is, he may conjecture that

$$P[y(t) = 1 \mid x = \xi] = P[y(t) = 1],$$
$$(\xi, t) \in \{0, 1, 2+\} \times \{a, b\}. \qquad (2.40)$$

The judge may want to use this exclusion restriction to choose sentences. However, combining assumption (2.40) with the empirical evidence shows that there exist no feasible values for the counterfactual outcomes. Hence, the assumption is incorrect and should not be used in treatment choice.

To see that the assumption is incorrect, let $t = a$. The linear equations (2.35) are

$$e_{a0}p_{a0} + \kappa_{\gamma a0}(1 - p_{a0}) = e_{a1}p_{a1} + \kappa_{\gamma a1}(1 - p_{a1})$$
$$= e_{a2}p_{a2} + \kappa_{\gamma a2}(1 - p_{a2}).$$

Inserting the empirically known values of

$$(e_{a0}, p_{a0}; e_{a1}, p_{a1}; e_{a2}, p_{a2})$$

yields

$$(0.52)(0.96) + \kappa_{\gamma a0}(0.04) = (0.30)(0.89) + \kappa_{\gamma a1}(0.11)$$
$$= (0.16)(0.73) + \kappa_{\gamma a2}(0.27).$$

Inspection of these equations shows that they hold for no values of $(\kappa_{\gamma a0}, \kappa_{\gamma a1}, \kappa_{\gamma a2})$ in the unit hypercube.

2.3.2   Monotone Instrumental Variables

The judge of the above illustration was fortunate to learn that his conjecture of mean-independence of prior referrals and future criminality is false. In many cases, the empirical evidence does not reveal when exclusion restrictions are incorrect. Then a planner contemplating use of such an assumption to choose treatments can do no more than introspect on the validity of the assumption. Although researchers have long used exclusion restrictions to analyze treatment response, they frequently have found these assumptions difficult to motivate. Planners are likely to encounter similar difficulties, so there is good reason to consider weaker assumptions that may be more credible.

When the set V of instrumental-variable values is ordered, one can sometimes enhance the credibility of an exclusion restriction by replacing the equalities in (2.34) with weak inequalities, as follows:

$$\nu'' > \nu' \ \Rightarrow \ E[u(t) \mid w, \ v = \nu'']$$
$$\geqslant E[u(t) \mid w, \ v = \nu'], \quad t \in T. \quad (2.41)$$

Covariate v is then termed a *monotone instrumental variable* (Manski and Pepper 2000). With (2.41) replacing (2.34), the argument yielding the linear equalities (2.35) now yields the linear inequalities

$$\nu'' > \nu' \ \Rightarrow \ e_{t(\omega,\nu'')}p_{t(\omega,\nu'')} + \kappa_{\gamma t(\omega,\nu'')}(1 - p_{t(\omega,\nu'')})$$
$$\geqslant e_{t(\omega,\nu')}p_{t(\omega,\nu')} + \kappa_{\gamma t(\omega,\nu')}(1 - p_{t(\omega,\nu')}).$$
$$(2.42)$$

Thus, the counterfactual values $(\kappa_{\gamma t \xi}, \ \xi \in X_\omega)$ are now jointly feasible if and only if they lie in the hyper-rectangle $\{[u_{0t\xi}, u_{1t\xi}], \ \xi \in X_\omega\}$ and satisfy the system of linear inequalities (2.42).

Although it is easy to state the implications for identification of monotone-instrumental-variable assumptions, their implications for treatment choice appear to be more complex to study than those of exclusion restrictions.

3
Treatment Using Experimental Data

To focus on the identification problem arising from the unobservability of counterfactual outcomes, Chapter 2 assumed that the planner knows the distribution $P(x, s, y)$ of (covariates, treatments, outcomes) in the study population. In practice, a planner may observe only a sample of the study population. This chapter and the next examine treatment choice with sample data.

This chapter builds on Manski (2004). Section 3.1 sets out general ideas, based on the Wald (1950) development of statistical decision theory. Sections 3.2 and 3.3 assume that the status quo treatment rule randomly allocated members of the study population across treatments, as in a classical experiment. Randomization implies that the response distributions $P[y(t) \mid x]$, $t \in T$, are point identified. Chapter 4 briefly examines treatment choice when a planner must contend with both the selection problem and the necessity of statistical inference from sample to population.

3.1 The Expected Welfare (Risk) of a Statistical Treatment Rule

To conceptualize treatment choice with sample data, we first need to generalize the concept of a treatment rule.

Statistical treatment rules map covariates and sample data into treatment allocations. Let Q denote the process generating sample data on the study population and let Ψ denote the sample space; that is, Ψ is the set of data samples that may be drawn under Q. Let Z henceforth denote the space of functions that map $T \times X \times \Psi$ into the unit interval and that satisfy the adding-up conditions:

$$z \in Z \;\Rightarrow\; \sum_{t \in T} z(t, \xi, \psi) = 1 \quad \forall (\xi, \psi) \in X \times \Psi.$$

Then each function $z \in Z$ defines a statistical treatment rule. The term *statistical treatment rule* adapts to treatment choice Wald's use of the more general term *statistical decision function* to describe functions that map sample data into decisions.

Wald proposed that alternative statistical decision functions be evaluated by their expected performance as the sampling process is engaged repeatedly to draw independent data samples. Considering situations in which the objective is to minimize expected loss, Wald called expected performance *risk*. Here the objective is to maximize population welfare, so I use the term *expected welfare* rather than risk.

Let z be any rule. Repeated engagement of the sampling process to draw independent samples makes population mean welfare a random variable. The expected welfare yielded by z in repeated samples is

$$W(z, P, Q)$$

$$\equiv \int \left\{ \sum_{\xi \in X} P(x = \xi) \sum_{t \in T} z(t, \xi, \psi) E[u(t) \mid x = \xi] \right\} dQ(\psi)$$

$$= \sum_{\xi \in X} P(x = \xi) \sum_{t \in T} E[z(t, \xi, \psi)] E[u(t) \mid x = \xi].$$

$$(3.1)$$

Here

$$E[z(t, \xi, \psi)] \equiv \int z(t, \xi, \psi) \, \mathrm{d}Q(\psi)$$

is the expected (across repeated samples) fraction of persons with covariates ξ who are assigned to treatment t. In the case of a singleton rule, the expected allocation to treatment t is the probability of drawing a sample in which z assigns all persons with covariates ξ to this treatment; that is, $E[z(t, \xi, \psi)] = Q[z(t, \xi, \psi) = 1]$.

3.1.1 Implementable Criteria for Treatment Choice

Maximization of expected welfare over Z yields the optimal treatment rule, but is not feasible without knowledge of P. To develop implementable criteria for treatment choice, let Γ again index the feasible states of nature. Thus, $[(P_\gamma, Q_\gamma), \ \gamma \in \Gamma]$ is the set of (P, Q) pairs that the planner deems possible. The present Γ is generically larger than the one considered in Chapter 2. There, Γ included only states of nature that are feasible given knowledge of $P(x, s, y)$. Here, the planner does not know $P(x, s, y)$ and must try to learn about the study population from sample data. However, I continue to assume that the planner knows the distribution $P(x)$ of covariate values. This is realistic because, from the beginning, we have presumed that the planner observes x for each member of the treatment population.

There is considerable consensus among statistical decision theorists that an action should not be chosen if it is weakly dominated in risk. A statistical treatment rule is weakly dominated in risk if there exists another feasible rule that yields at least the same expected welfare in all feasible states of nature, and larger expected welfare in some state of nature. Thus, rule z is weakly dominated if there exists another rule, say z', such that $W(z', P_\gamma, Q_\gamma) \geqslant W(z, P_\gamma, Q_\gamma)$ for all $\gamma \in \Gamma$ and $W(z', P_\gamma, Q_\gamma) > W(z, P_\gamma, Q_\gamma)$ for some $\gamma \in \Gamma$.

There is no similar consensus on choice among undominated actions, but the same two broad ideas that were discussed in Chapter 2 have been prominent: one might choose a rule that works well on average or one that works well uniformly over Γ. A Bayesian planner places a subjective probability measure π on Γ and solves the optimization problem

$$\sup_{z \in Z} \int W(z, P_\gamma, Q_\gamma) \, d\pi(\gamma). \tag{3.2}$$

Solution of this problem, which views treatment rules as procedures, differs in concept but agrees in practice with the perhaps more familiar *conditional Bayes* prescription for decision-making. The latter calls on the planner to form a posterior subjective distribution on Γ, conditional on the sample data, and to maximize the expected value of $U(z, P)$ with respect to this posterior distribution. Although the two problems differ, solution of the latter problem at all points in the sample space yields the solution to the former (see Berger 1985, Section 4.4.1).

The finite-sample maximin criterion is

$$\sup_{z \in Z} \inf_{\gamma \in \Gamma} W(z, P_\gamma, Q_\gamma) \tag{3.3}$$

and the finite-sample minimax-regret criterion is

$$\inf_{z \in Z} \sup_{\gamma \in \Gamma} U^*(P_\gamma) - W(z, P_\gamma, Q_\gamma). \tag{3.4}$$

Here, as in Chapter 2, $U^*(P_\gamma)$ is the optimal population mean welfare that would be achievable if it were known that $P = P_\gamma$:

$$U^*(P_\gamma) \equiv \sum_{\xi \in X} P(x = \xi)$$

$$\times \left\{ \max_{t \in T} \int u[y(t), t, \xi] \, \mathrm{d}P_\gamma[y(t) \mid x = \xi] \right\}.$$
$$(3.5)$$

3.1.2 Discussion

Wald's statistical decision theory may be applied whenever expected welfare $W(\cdot, \cdot, \cdot)$ exists on its domain $Z \times [(P_\gamma, Q_\gamma), \ \gamma \in \Gamma]$. In principle, the theory enables comparison of all feasible statistical treatment rules. It applies whatever the sampling process may be and whatever information the planner may have about the population and the sampling process.

Wald's theory also enables comparison of alternative sampling processes. Consider a two-period world, with data collected from a study population in the first period and treatment choices made in the second. A planner may want to jointly choose a sampling process and a treatment rule that uses the data generated by this process. Let $C(Q)$ denote the cost of sampling process Q, with cost measured in the same units as welfare. The expected welfare of (treatment rule, sampling process) pair (z, Q) is then $W(z, P, Q) - C(Q)$. Section 3.3 illustrates how the finite-sample minimax-regret criterion can be used to choose a sample design.

Observe that Wald's theory addresses the problem of finite-sample statistical inference directly, without recourse to the large-sample approximations of asymptotic statistical theory. Indeed, the concept of regret provides a decision theoretic foundation for the development of asymptotic theory. Consider a commensurate sequence of sampling processes and treatment rules

$(z_N, Q_N; N = 1, \ldots, \infty)$, where N indexes sample size. This sequence is pointwise consistent if regret converges to zero in all states of nature, and uniformly consistent if maximum regret converges to zero. Thus, the sequence $(z_N, Q_N; N = 1, \ldots, \infty)$ is pointwise consistent if $\lim_{N \to \infty} U^*(P_\gamma) - W(z_N, P_\gamma, Q_N) = 0$, for all $\gamma \in \Gamma$. It is uniformly consistent if $\lim_{N \to \infty} \{ \sup_{\gamma \in \Gamma} U^*(P_\gamma) - W(z_N, P_\gamma, Q_N) \} = 0$.

The primary conceptual criticism of Wald has been the conditional Bayes argument that statistical inference should be based only on observed data and not on frequentist thought experiments that contemplate how a procedure would perform in repeated sampling. Thus, decision theorists of the conditional Bayes school argue that risk is not an appropriate measure of the performance of a statistical decision function (see, for example, Berger 1985, Chapter 1). Contrariwise, frequentists have observed with discomfort that the Bayesian approach requires assertion of a subjective prior distribution on unknown states of nature. Some researchers have sought to blend aspects of Bayesian and frequentist thinking (e.g. Samaniego and Reneau 1994; Chamberlain 2000). The continuing doctrinal debates between and within the frequentist and Bayesian schools of thought will not be settled here.

Apart from the conditional Bayes criticism of frequentist statistics, the primary impediment to use of Wald's statistical decision theory has been computational rather than conceptual. Early on, statistical decision theorists found that it can be difficult to determine what actions are dominated and to solve the optimization problems yielding a Bayes, minimax (here maximin), or minimax-regret action. As a consequence, the surge of decision theoretic research that immediately followed publication of Wald (1950) did not endure. Of course, conclusions about computational tractability drawn 50 years ago may not be entirely relevant today. Hence, the practicality of Wald's theory warrants a fresh appraisal. This chapter and the next take steps in this direction.

3.2 Using a Randomized Experiment to Evaluate an Innovation

This section examines what may be the simplest nontrivial case of treatment choice using sample data. Outcomes are binary, there are no observed covariates, and there are two treatments: the status quo and an innovation. The planner knows the response distribution of the status quo treatment, but not that of the innovation. To learn about the innovation, an experiment with a randomized treatment assignment is performed. The objective is to use the experimental data to inform treatment choice.

A theorem of Karlin and Rubin (1956) shows that, in this setting, the undominated treatment rules coincide with the *monotone treatment rules*. These are rules which assign all persons to the status quo treatment if the experimental success rate is below some threshold, and all to the innovation treatment if the success rate is above the threshold. Observing that the class of monotone treatment rules is mathematically "small" but substantively "large," I go on to examine various rules within this class. The minimax-regret rule is particularly appealing. This rule solves a sensible, objective, optimization problem and makes judicious use of sample data.

3.2.1 The Setting

There are two treatments, a binary outcome, and no observed covariates; thus, $T = \{a, b\}$, $Y = \{0, 1\}$, and

$X = \phi$. One treatment, say $t = a$, is the status quo and the other, $t = b$, is an innovation. The planner knows the response distribution $P[y(a)]$ of the status quo treatment, perhaps through observation of historical experience. The planner does not know the response distribution $P[y(b)]$ of the innovation. I suppose that welfare is the outcome of a treatment; that is, $u[y_j(t), t, x_j] = y_j(t)$. In the present setting—with a binary outcome, no covariates, and $P[y(a)]$ known—this is a normalization rather than a substantive assumption.

An experiment is performed to learn about outcomes under the innovation, with N subjects randomly drawn from the population and assigned to treatment b. Of these subjects, a number n realize outcome $y = 1$ and the remaining $N - n$ realize outcome $y = 0$. The outcomes of all subjects are observed.

In this setting, the sample size N indexes the sampling process, and the number n of experimental successes is a sufficient statistic for the sample data. The feasible statistical treatment rules are functions $z : T \times [0, \dots, N] \rightarrow [0, 1]$ that map the number of experimental successes into a treatment allocation; that is, for each value of n, rule z randomly allocates a fraction $z(b, n)$ of the population to treatment b and the remaining $z(a, n) = 1 - z(b, n)$ to treatment a.

Let $p(t) \equiv P[y(t) = 1]$, $t \in T$. The expected welfare of rule z is

$$W(z, P, N) = p(a)E[z(a, n)] + p(b)E[z(b, n)]$$
$$= p(a) + [p(b) - p(a)]E[z(b, n)]. \qquad (3.6)$$

The number of experimental successes is distributed binomial, $\boldsymbol{B}[p(b), N]$, so

$$E[z(b, n)] = \sum_{i=0}^{N} z(b, i) f[n = i; p(b), N], \qquad (3.7)$$

where

$$f[n = i; p(b), N] \equiv N![i!(N - i)!]^{-1}p(b)^i[1 - p(b)]^{N-i}$$

is the binomial probability of i successes.

The only unknown determinant of expected welfare is $p(b)$. Hence, Γ indexes the feasible values of $p(b)$. I presume that $[p_\gamma(b), \ \gamma \in \Gamma]$ contains values that are smaller and larger than $p(a)$; otherwise, the choice problem is trivial.

Although our main interest is in using experimental evidence to inform treatment choice, the present analysis also covers the case of $N = 0$, in which no experiment is performed. Indeed, this case was the subject of a famous thought experiment by Ellsberg (1961). Ellsberg contemplated how a person would choose when required to draw a ball from one of two urns, each containing balls of two colors, say red and blue. The person is told the composition of balls in one urn but has no knowledge of the composition of the other urn. He receives a reward if he draws a red ball but nothing if he draws a blue ball. In the language of this section, the former urn is the status quo treatment, whose probability of success is known, and the latter is the innovation, whose probability of success is unknown.

3.2.2 *Undominated Treatment Rules*

In the setting described above, larger values of n are evidence for larger values of $p(b)$. Hence, it is reasonable to conjecture that undominated treatment rules should be ones in which the share $z(b, \cdot)$ of the population allocated to treatment b increases with n. In fact, the undominated treatment rules are a simple subclass of these rules.

Define a *monotone treatment rule* to be one of the form

$$z(b, n) = \begin{cases} 0 & \text{for } n < n_0, \\ \lambda & \text{for } n = n_0, \\ 1 & \text{for } n > n_0, \end{cases} \tag{3.8}$$

where $0 \leqslant n_0 \leqslant N$ and $0 \leqslant \lambda \leqslant 1$. Thus, a monotone rule allocates all persons to treatment a if n is smaller than the specified threshold n_0, a fraction λ to treatment b if $n = n_0$, and all persons to treatment b if n is larger than n_0. Observe that monotone rules have simple expressions for the expected treatment allocation, namely

$$E[z(b, n)] = f[n > n_0; p(b), N] + \lambda f[n = n_0; p(b), N]. \tag{3.9}$$

The result is given in the following proposition.

Proposition 3.1. *Let* $0 < p(a) < 1$ *and let the feasible set* $[p_\gamma(b), \ \gamma \in \Gamma]$ *exclude the values 0 and 1. Then the collection of monotone treatment rules is the set of undominated rules.*

Proof. This is an application of Karlin and Rubin (1956, Theorem 4). The Karlin and Rubin theorem concerns the class of decision problems with three features. First, there are two feasible actions. Second, the unknown state of nature is real valued and there exists a unique interior *change point* such that one action has better risk under states of nature lower than the change point, and the other has better risk under states of nature higher than the change point. Third, the sample data are the realization of a real random variable whose density function (with respect to some σ-finite measure) has the strict form of the monotone likelihood ratio property.

In the present setting, the two actions are choice of treatment a or b. The unknown state of nature is $p(b)$ and the change point is $p(a)$; treatment a is better in

state of nature γ if $p_\gamma(b) < p(a)$ and treatment b is
better if $p_\gamma(b) > p(a)$. The sample data are the realization of n, whose binomial distribution has density
with respect to counting measure. This density function,
namely $f[n; p_\gamma(b), N]$, has the strict form of the monotone likelihood ratio property. That is,

$i > i'$ and $p_\gamma(b) > p_{\gamma'}(b)$

$$\Rightarrow \quad \frac{f[n = i; p_\gamma(b), N]}{f[n = i'; p_\gamma(b), N]} > \frac{f[n = i; p_{\gamma'}(b), N]}{f[n = i'; p_{\gamma'}(b), N]}.$$

Thus, the theorem applies here.   □

A weaker version of the theorem holds if $p(a)$ or $p(b)$
can take the value 0 or 1. Then, Karlin and Rubin (1956,
Theorem 1) show that the collection of monotone treatment rules is *essentially complete*. That is, given any non-
monotone rule z', there exists a monotone rule z such
that $W(z, P_\gamma, N) \geqslant W(z', P_\gamma, N)$, $\forall \gamma \in \Gamma$ (see Berger
(1985, Section 8.3) for an exposition of the Karlin–Rubin
theorems and related findings).

3.2.3   Some Monotone Rules

The collection of monotone treatment rules is a mathematically "small" but substantively "large" subset of the
space of all feasible treatment rules. This collection of
rules is mathematically small in that it excludes almost
all feasible rules, in the sense of Lebesgue measure. The
space of all feasible rules is the Cartesian product of
N replicates of the unit simplex in $\mathbb{R}^2$. Whereas this
space has positive Lebesgue measure, the collection of
monotone rules has Lebesgue measure zero.

To demonstrate that the collection of monotone rules
is substantively large, I describe various forms that such
a rule may take.

Data-Invariant Rules

These are the rules $z(b, \cdot) = 0$ and $z(b, \cdot) = 1$, which assign all persons to treatment a or b, respectively, whatever the realization of n may be.

Empirical Success Rules

An optimal treatment rule allocates all persons to treatment a if $p(b) < p(a)$ and all to treatment b if $p(b) > p(a)$. An empirical success rule emulates the optimal rule by replacing $p(b)$ with its sample analog, the empirical success rate, n/N. Thus, an empirical success rule has the form

$$z(b, n) = \begin{cases} 0 & \text{for } n < p(a)N, \\ \lambda & \text{for } n = p(a)N, \text{ where } 0 \leqslant \lambda \leqslant 1, \\ 1 & \text{for } n > p(a)N. \end{cases}$$

$$(3.10)$$

Bayes Rules

A planner who commits to using a Bayes rule has enormous discretion, because the form of the Bayes rule depends critically on the prior subjective distribution placed on $p(b)$. To see this, consider the class of beta priors, which form the conjugate family for a binomial likelihood. Let $[p_\gamma(b), \ \gamma \in \Gamma] = (0, 1)$ and let the prior be beta with parameters (α, β). The posterior mean for $p(b)$ is then $(\alpha + n)/(\alpha + \beta + N)$ (see, for example, DeGroot 1970, Section 9.2, Theorem 1). The resulting Bayes rule is

$$z(b, n) = \begin{cases} 0 & \text{for } (\alpha + n)/(\alpha + \beta + N) < p(a), \\ \lambda & \text{for } (\alpha + n)/(\alpha + \beta + N) = p(a), \\ 1 & \text{for } (\alpha + n)/(\alpha + \beta + N) > p(a). \end{cases}$$

$$(3.11)$$

where $0 \leqslant \lambda \leqslant 1$. As (α, β) tend to zero, the Bayes rule approaches an empirical success rule. Moreover, the class of Bayes rules includes the data-invariant rules $z(b, \cdot) = 0$ and $z(b, \cdot) = 1$. The former occurs if the parameters (α, β) of the beta prior distribution satisfy

$$\frac{\alpha + N}{\alpha + \beta + N} < p(a).$$

The latter occurs if

$$\frac{\alpha}{\alpha + \beta + N} > p(a).$$

Statistical Significance Rules

These rules use a one-sided hypothesis test to choose between the status quo treatment and the innovation. The null hypothesis is that both treatments yield the same mean welfare; that is, $p(b) = p(a)$. The alternative is that treatment b is superior to treatment a; that is, $p(b) > p(a)$. Treatment b is chosen if the null is rejected, and treatment a is chosen otherwise. Thus, the rule is

$$z(b, n) = \begin{cases} 0 & \text{for } n \leqslant d[\alpha, p(a), N], \\ 1 & \text{for } n > d[\alpha, p(a), N], \end{cases} \tag{3.12}$$

where α is the specified size of the test and $d[\alpha, p(a), N]$ is the associated critical value. Given that n is binomial, $d[\alpha, p(a), N] = \min i : f[n > i; p(a), N] \leqslant \alpha$.

Although statistical significance rules are monotone treatment rules, the conventional practice of hypothesis testing is remote from the problem of treatment choice with sample data. If the null hypothesis

$$H_0 : [p(b) = p(a)]$$

is correct, all feasible treatment rules yield the same expected welfare. If not, alternative rules may yield different expected welfare. A statistical test of H_0 indicates only whether the sample data are inconsistent (in the usual sense of having low probability of being realized under the null) with the hypothesis that all feasible rules yield the same expected welfare.

The Finite-Sample Maximin Rule

The finite-sample maximin criterion yields a specific data-invariant rule. The infimum of expected welfare for rule z is

$$\inf_{\gamma \in \Gamma} W(z, P_\gamma, N) = p(a) + \min_{\gamma \in \Gamma}[p_\gamma(b) - p(a)]E_\gamma[z(b, n)],$$
(3.13)

where $E_\gamma[z(b, n)]$ is the expression in (3.9) with $p_\gamma(b)$ replacing $p(b)$. By assumption, $[p_\gamma(b), \gamma \in \Gamma]$ contains values that are smaller than $p(a)$. Moreover, $E_\gamma[z(b, n)] > 0$ for all $p_\gamma(b) > 0$ and all monotone treatment rules except for $z(b, \cdot) = 0$, the rule that always chooses treatment a. Hence, the maximin rule is $z(b, \cdot) = 0$.

The Finite-Sample Minimax-Regret Rule

The regret of rule z in state of nature γ is

$$
\begin{aligned}
U^*&(P_\gamma) - W(z, P_\gamma, N) \\
&= \max[p(a), p_\gamma(b)] \\
&\quad - \{p(a) + [p_\gamma(b) - p(a)]E_\gamma[z(b, n)]\} \\
&= \begin{cases} [p_\gamma(b) - p(a)]E_\gamma[z(a, n)] & \text{if } p_\gamma(b) \geqslant p(a), \\ [p(a) - p_\gamma(b)]E_\gamma[z(b, n)] & \text{if } p(a) \geqslant p_\gamma(b). \end{cases}
\end{aligned}
$$
(3.14)

Thus, regret is the mean welfare loss when a member of the population is assigned the inferior treatment, multiplied by the expected fraction of the population assigned this treatment.

The minimax-regret rule can be determined numerically. The maximum regret of rule z is

$$R(z) \equiv \sup_{\gamma \in \Gamma} [p_\gamma(b) - p(a)] E_\gamma[z(a, n)] \mathbf{1}[p_\gamma(b) \geqslant p(a)]$$

$$+ [p(a) - p_\gamma(b)] E_\gamma[z(b, n)] \mathbf{1}[p(a) \geqslant p_\gamma(b)].$$
$$(3.15)$$

The expressions

$$[p_\gamma(b) - p(a)] E_\gamma[z(a, n)] \quad \text{and} \quad [p(a) - p_\gamma(b)] E_\gamma[z(b, n)]$$

are $(N + 1)$-order polynomials in $p_\gamma(b)$. The maximum regret of rule z is obtained by maximizing the first polynomial over $\{\gamma : p_\gamma(b) \geqslant p(a)\}$, the second over $\{\gamma : p(a) \geqslant p_\gamma(b)\}$, and selecting the larger of the two maxima. The minimax-regret rule is then obtained by minimizing $R(\cdot)$ over the collection of monotone treatment rules defined in (3.8), which are indexed by the threshold sample sizes and allocations (n_0, λ), $n_0 = 0, \ldots, N$, $\lambda \in [0, 1]$.

Table 3.1 reports the minimax-regret rule for specified values of $p(a)$ and N when all values of $p(b)$ are feasible; that is, when $[p_\gamma(b), \gamma \in \Gamma] = [0, 1]$. The top two panels display the value of (n_0, λ) for this rule. The third panel displays the value of minimax regret; that is, $R \equiv \min_{z \in Z} R(z)$. The bottom panel displays the state of nature at which R is achieved; this value is denoted $p_R(b)$.

Consider first the entries for $N = 0$, indicating the absence of sample data. In this case, the only feasible treatment rules are

$$[z(a, 0), z(b, 0)] = (1 - \lambda, \lambda) \in [0, 1].$$

For each value of λ, maximum regret is

$$\max\{[1 - p(a)](1 - \lambda), p(a)\lambda\}.$$

Hence, the minimax-regret rule is $[n_0 = 0, \ \lambda = 1 - p(a)]$ and the value of minimax regret is $R = p(a)[1 - p(a)]$. The rule allocates a positive fraction of the population to treatment b even if no experimental data are available; the magnitude of λ rises from 0 to 1 as $p(a)$ falls from 1 to 0.

The top panel of the table shows that the threshold n_0 of experimental successes for allocation of persons to treatment b increases with the sample size and with the success probability of treatment a. The inequality $|n_0 - p(a)N| \leqslant 1$ holds everywhere in the table. Thus, the minimax-regret rule is well approximated by an empirical success rule.

The second panel shows that randomization when n_0 successes are observed is a generic feature of the minimax-regret rule. The third panel shows that the value of minimax regret decreases by roughly an order of magnitude as the sample size increases from 0 to 10. The specific pattern of decrease varies markedly with the value of $p(a)$. A curiosity is that R is a step function when $p(a) = 0.5$, with decreases occurring at odd values, but not at even values, of N.

The bottom panel shows the state of nature $p_R(b)$ that maximizes regret for the minimax-regret rule. This state of nature locates the maximum of an $(N+1)$-order polynomial within the unit interval. Observe that $p_R(b)$ may be an extreme state of nature when $N \leqslant 3$, but is always an interior value when $N \geqslant 4$. When $p(a) = 0.50$, the polynomial is symmetric and so has two global maxima that are equidistant from 0.50.

3.2.4 *Savage on the Finite-Sample Maximin and Minimax-Regret Criteria*

The findings in Table 3.1 make it plain that treatment choice using the finite-sample minimax-regret rule differs

Table 3.1. Minimax-regret treatment rules.

$p(a)$	$N=0$	$N=1$	$N=2$	$N=3$	$N=4$	$N=5$	$N=6$	$N=7$	$N=8$	$N=9$	$N=10$
0.10	0	0	0	0	0	0	0	0	0	1	1
0.25	0	0	0	1	1	1	1	2	2	2	2
0.50	1	1	1	2	2	3	3	4	4	5	5
0.75	1	1	2	2	3	4	5	5	6	7	8
0.90	1	1	2	3	4	5	6	7	8	8	9
0.9	0.67	0.52	0.41	0.32	0.26	0.18	0.09	0	0.89	0.78	
0.75	0.36	0.17	0.93	0.67	0.42	0.18	0.93	0.67	0.43	0.18	
0.5	1	0.5	1	0.5	1	0.5	1	0.5	1	0.5	
0.25	0.64	0.83	0.07	0.33	0.58	0.82	0.07	0.33	0.57	0.82	
0.1	0.33	0.48	0.59	0.68	0.74	0.82	0.91	1	0.11	0.22	

Upper panel: N against $p(a)$ for n_0 (threshold sample size);
lower panel: N against $p(a)$ for λ (threshold allocation).

Table 3.1. *Cont.*

$p(a)$	$N=0$	$N=1$	$N=2$	$N=3$	$N=4$	$N=5$	$N=6$	$N=7$	$N=8$	$N=9$	$N=10$
0.10	0.09	0.067	0.052	0.041	0.033	0.027	0.022	0.019	0.017	0.017	0.017
0.25	0.19	0.09	0.052	0.039	0.038	0.035	0.03	0.027	0.027	0.025	0.023
0.50	0.25	0.063	0.063	0.044	0.044	0.035	0.035	0.03	0.03	0.027	0.027
0.75	0.19	0.09	0.052	0.039	0.038	0.035	0.03	0.027	0.027	0.025	0.023
0.90	0.09	0.067	0.052	0.041	0.033	0.027	0.022	0.019	0.017	0.017	0.016
0.10	0, 1	0	0	0	0.28	0.01	0.23	0.21	0.05	0.05	0.2
0.25	0, 1	0	0.5	0.45	0.45	0.42	0.4	0.15	0.38	0.15	0.36
0.50	0, 1	0.25	0.25	0.32	0.32	0.35	0.35	0.37	0.37	0.38	0.38
		0.75	0.75	0.68	0.68	0.65	0.65	0.63	0.63	0.62	0.62
0.75	0, 1	1	0.5	0.55	0.55	0.58	0.6	0.85	0.62	0.85	0.64
0.90	0, 1	1	1	1	0.72	0.99	0.77	0.79	0.95	0.95	0.8

Upper panel: N against $p(a)$ for R (minimax-regret value);
lower panel: N against $p(a)$ for $p_R(b)$ (regret state).

fundamentally from treatment choice using the maximin rule. Savage (1951), whose review of Wald (1950)
first distinguished explicitly between these criteria for
decision-making, argued strongly against application of
the minimax (here maximin) criterion, writing:

> Application of the minimax rule... is indeed
> ultra-pessimistic; no serious justification for
> it has ever been suggested, and it can lead to
> the absurd conclusion in some cases that no
> amount of relevant experimentation should
> deter the actor from behaving as though he
> were in complete ignorance.
>
> (Savage 1951, p. 63)

Our finding that the maximin treatment rule is data-
invariant illustrates this "absurd conclusion." Savage
emphasized that the ultra-pessimism of the minimax criterion is not shared by the minimax-regret criterion. Our
finding that the minimax-regret rule approximates the
empirical success rule illustrates that the minimax-regret
criterion is not particularly pessimistic.

Savage conjectured that Wald (1950), whose abstract
study of minimax principles encompasses both criteria,
had minimax regret in mind rather than minimax. However, Savage later reported (Savage 1954, Chapter 9)
that, in oral communication, Wald disavowed this notion
and credited the minimax-regret idea to Savage.

3.3   Using Covariate Information with Data from a Randomized Experiment

This section considers how best to use covariate information in treatment choice. The sample data are the realizations of an experiment randomly assigning subjects
to each feasible treatment. An experiment of unlimited

size would enable the planner to implement the optimal treatment rule, which conditions treatment choice on all observed covariates. The question of interest is treatment choice when the data are from an experiment with a finite sample of subjects. I address this question from the finite-sample minimax-regret perspective.

Researchers have long thought that it may not be judicious to condition predictions of outcomes on all observed covariates when the available sample is small, because estimates of best predictors tend to be less precise as the degree of conditioning increases. Statisticians studying prediction under square loss have used statistical decision theory to motivate *shrinkage estimators* (see, for example, Copas 1983; Lehmann 1983, Section 4.6) and *variable selection procedures* (see, for example, Kempthorne 1984; Droge 1998). The statistical literature on prediction with sample data is important, but its findings do not appear to hold specific lessons for treatment choice. The reason is that prediction to minimize the expected value of square loss and treatment choice to maximize a utilitarian social welfare function are rather different mathematical problems.

A complete analysis would first determine the set of undominated treatment rules and then consider choice among the undominated rules. This does not appear to be practical, but restriction of our attention to a tractable class of treatment rules makes progress possible. In particular, I consider the family of *conditional empirical success* (CES) rules; these rules select treatments that maximize sample-average outcomes conditional on specified subsets of the observed covariates.

When there are two treatments, a large-deviations theorem of Hoeffding (1963) implies a closed-form bound on the maximum regret of any CES rule. These bounds imply *sufficient sample sizes* for the beneficial use of covariate information. When the available sample size exceeds the sufficiency boundary, a planner can be certain that conditioning treatment choice on the observed covariates is preferable (in terms of minimax regret) to not conditioning.

3.3.1   The Setting

A randomized experiment is performed in order to learn about treatment response, and the outcomes of all subjects are observed. I consider two experimental designs: stratified and simple random sampling. These designs are polar cases, the former with the greatest feasible degree of stratification and the latter with the least. The proposition on simple random sampling developed below can be modified to cover intermediate cases, in which the design stratifies on some but not all covariates.

Stratified Random Sampling

The experimenter assigns to each treatment a specified number of subjects with each value of the covariates. Thus, for $(t, \xi) \in T \times X$, the experimenter draws $N_{t\xi}$ subjects at random from the subpopulation with covariates ξ and assigns them to treatment t. The set

$$N_{TX} \equiv [N_{t\xi}, \ (t, \xi) \in T \times X]$$

of stratum sample sizes indexes the sampling process. For each $(t, \xi) \in T \times X$, let $N(t, \xi)$ be the subsample of subjects with covariates ξ who are assigned to treatment t. Then the sample data are the outcomes

$$Y_{TX} \equiv [y_j, \ j \in N(t, \xi); \ (t, \xi) \in T \times X].$$

The feasible rules are functions that map covariates and the data into a treatment allocation. Thus, for each $\xi \in X$ and Y_{TX}, rule z randomly allocates a fraction

$z(t, \xi, Y_{TX})$ of persons with covariates ξ to treatment t. The expected welfare of rule z is

$$W(z, P, N_{TX})$$
$$= \sum_{\xi \in X} P(x = \xi) \sum_{t \in T} E[u(t) \mid x = \xi] E[z(t, \xi, Y_{TX})].$$

$$(3.16)$$

Simple Random Sampling

The experimenter draws N subjects at random from the population and randomly assigns them to treatments with specified assignment probabilities, say $q \equiv (q_t,\ t \in T)$. The pair (N, q) indexes the sampling process. The sample data are the stratum sample sizes N_{TX} and the outcomes Y_{TX}. Rule z allocates a fraction $z(t, \xi, N_{TX}, Y_{TX})$ of persons with covariates ξ to treatment t. The expected welfare of rule z is

$$W(z, P, N, q)$$
$$= \sum_{\xi \in X} P(x = \xi) \sum_{t \in T} E[u(t) \mid x = \xi] E[z(t, \xi, N_{TX}, Y_{TX})].$$

$$(3.17)$$

CES Rules

Comparison of all feasible treatment rules appears impractical. Instead, I restrict my attention to a tractable class of rules. Statisticians studying estimation have long made progress by restricting their attention to tractable classes of estimators; for example, linear unbiased or asymptotic normal ones. Similarly, I make progress here by restricting my attention to *conditional empirical success* rules.

An empirical success rule emulates the optimal treatment rule by replacing unknown response distributions with sample analogs. The optimal rule solves the problems $\max_{t \in T} E[u(t) \mid x = \xi]$, $\xi \in X$. An empirical success rule replaces $E[u(t) \mid x = \xi]$ by a corresponding sample average and chooses treatments that maximize empirical success. Let $u_j \equiv u(y_j, t, \xi)$. Then $E[u(t) \mid x = \xi]$ is replaced by $\bar{u}_{t\xi} \equiv (1/N_{t\xi}) \sum_{j \in N(t,\xi)} u_j$ and an empirical success rule solves the problems $\max_{t \in T} \bar{u}_{t\xi}$, $\xi \in X$.

The above rule conditions treatment choice on all observed covariates, as is optimal when the distribution of treatment response is known. However, conditioning tends to diminish the statistical precision of the sample averages used to estimate population means. Hence, conditioning on some part of the observed covariates may be preferable when making treatment choices with sample data. This suggests comparison of empirical success rules that condition on alternative subsets of the observed covariates. Formally, let $v(\cdot) : X \to V$ map the covariate space X into a space V. Then a conditional empirical success rule chooses treatments that maximize empirical success conditional on a person's value of v.

The proper way to measure empirical success conditional on v depends on the experimental design. Let $\nu \in V$. In a design with simple random sampling, the appropriate sample analog of $E[u(t) \mid v = \nu]$ is

$$\bar{u}_{t\nu} \equiv \frac{1}{N_{t\nu}} \sum_{j \in N(t,\nu)} u_j,$$

where $N(t, \nu)$ is the subsample of subjects with covariates ν who are assigned to treatment t, and where $N_{t\nu} \equiv |N(t,\nu)|$. In a design with stratified random sampling, the appropriate sample analog is the design-weighted average

$$\bar{u}_{tX\nu} \equiv \sum_{\xi \in X} \bar{u}_{t\xi} P(x = \xi \mid v = \nu).$$

In an x-stratified design, $\bar{u}_{t\xi}$ is the sample analog of $E[u(t) \mid x = \xi]$, but $\bar{u}_{tv}$ is not that of $E[u(t) \mid v = \nu]$. However, the Law of Iterated Expectations gives

$$E[u(t) \mid v = \nu] = \sum_{\xi \in X} E[u(t) \mid x = \xi] P(x = \xi \mid v = \nu).$$

Hence, $\bar{u}_{tXv}$ is the sample analog of $E[u(t) \mid v = \nu]$.

Let z_{Xv} denote the CES rule conditioning on v in a design with stratified random sampling, and let z_v denote the corresponding rule in a design with simple random sampling. If outcomes are continuously distributed, expected welfare is given by

$$W(z_{Xv}, P, N_{TX}) = \sum_{\nu \in V} P(v = \nu) \sum_{t \in T} E[u(t) \mid v = \nu]$$
$$\times P(\bar{u}_{tXv} \geqslant \bar{u}_{t'Xv}, \ t' \in T) \quad (3.18)$$

in a design with stratified random sampling and

$$W(z_v, P, N, q)$$
$$= \sum_{\nu \in V} P(v = \nu) \sum_{t \in T} E[u(t) \mid v = \nu] P(\bar{u}_{tv} \geqslant \bar{u}_{t'v}, \ t' \in T)$$
$$(3.19)$$

in one with simple random sampling. If outcomes have discrete distributions, a tie-breaking convention is required to determine treatment choice when multiple treatments maximize empirical success.

3.3.2 Empirical Illustration: Alternative Rules for Treatment of Hypertension

To illustrate the performance of alternative CES rules, I examine a scenario concerning pharmaceutical treatments for hypertension. Medicine provides especially apt illustrations of the potential use of covariate information in treatment choice. Physicians are well aware that response to treatment may vary across patients, and they often observe many covariates for their patients. Physicians routinely read the empirical findings of randomized clinical trials (RCTs) that report sample evidence on treatment response.

Heterogeneity in treatment response has been an important theme of medical research on hypertension, which holds that "Antihypertensive treatment must be tailored to the individual patient" (Materson et al. 1993, p. 919). The Materson et al. article aimed to learn how treatment response varies with the race and age of the patient; the authors categorized patients less than 60 years old as "younger" and others as "older." The authors presented findings from an RCT of treatments for hypertension.

Male patients were randomly assigned one of six antihypertensive drug treatments or a placebo: hydrochlorothiazide ($t = 1$), atenolol ($t = 2$), captopril ($t = 3$), clonidine ($t = 4$), diltiazem ($t = 5$), prazosin ($t = 6$), placebo ($t = 7$). The trial had two phases. In the first, the dosage that brought diastolic blood pressure (DBP) below 90 mm Hg was determined. In the second, it was determined whether DBP could be kept below 95 mm Hg for a long time. Treatment was defined to be successful if DBP $<$ 90 mm Hg on two consecutive measurement occasions in the first phase and DBP $\leqslant$ 95 mm Hg in the second. Treatment was deemed unsuccessful otherwise. Thus the outcome of interest was binary, with $y(t) = 1$ if the criterion for success was met and $y(t) = 0$ otherwise. Taking $y(t)$ to fully represent the outcome of interest is an idealization. In fact, Materson et al. (1993) recommended that physicians making treatment choices should consider this medical outcome variable in addition to patient's quality of life and the cost of treatment.

Table 3.2. Success rates and sample sizes, by age and race. (DG, demographic group; YB, younger blacks; OB, older blacks; YW, younger whites; OW, older whites.)

	Treatment							
	1		2		3		4	
DG	$\bar{y}_{x1}$	N_{x1}	$\bar{y}_{x2}$	N_{x2}	$\bar{y}_{x3}$	N_{x3}	$\bar{y}_{x4}$	N_{x4}
YB	0.48	48	0.51	35	0.43	44	0.48	40
OB	0.64	44	0.45	47	0.33	48	0.58	45
YW	0.32	34	0.65	37	0.62	39	0.69	32
OW	0.68	60	0.72	58	0.62	55	0.73	60

	5		6		7	
DG	$\bar{y}_{x5}$	N_{x5}	$\bar{y}_{x6}$	N_{x6}	$\bar{y}_{x7}$	N_{x7}
YB	0.70	37	0.42	43	0.23	44
OB	0.85	53	0.49	49	0.27	44
YW	0.58	40	0.55	33	0.26	31
OW	0.72	53	0.69	58	0.38	64

There were no missing data on the race and age covariates. The authors performed an intention-to-treat analysis that interpreted attrition from the trial as lack of success; from this perspective there were no missing outcome data either. Thus, this RCT may be viewed as a classical randomized experiment with complete observation of sample realizations.

Table 3.2 presents the revised findings reported in Figure 2 of Materson, Reda, and Cushman (1995), correcting a computational error in the original article. Analyzing the data in Table 3.2, Materson et al. (1995, p. 189) summarized this way: "Whites responded well to all drug classes, except for lower efficacy of hydrochlorothiazide

in younger whites. Blacks responded better to diltiazem
than other agents." They did not make specific recommendations for treatment choice but concluded (Materson et al. 1995, p. 192): "there were important age-by-
race differences in success rates that can assist the clin-
ician in selection of an effective drug for an individual
patient." Thus, the authors gently suggest that physicians may want to condition their treatment choices on
patient age and race.

Consider a physician who accepts the binary success
criterion, who observes the race and age of his patients,
and who wants to choose treatments in a population with
the same (covariate, response) distribution as the study
population. This physician could use the study findings
to implement any one of four CES rules: rule z_{RA}, which
conditions treatment choice on (race, age); rule z_R, which
conditions only on race; rule z_A, which conditions only
on age; and rule $z_\emptyset$, which requires uniform treatment
of all persons. If the sample size were to be infinite, the
physician should choose rule z_{RA}. However, the total size
of the sample was $N = 1275$ and, as shown in Table 3.2,
the subsamples of subjects with particular (covariate,
treatment) values range in size from 31 to 64. These
subsample sizes are sufficiently small as to make sampling variation a relevant consideration in interpreting
the empirical findings.

Table 3.3 reports computations of the treatment-selection probabilities and expected welfare of the four alternative empirical success rules under the assumption that
Table 3.2 gives the population distribution of treatment
response and covariates. Thus, for $v \in (RA, R, A, \emptyset)$,
Table 3.3 gives $Q_N[\bar{y}_{vt} \geqslant \bar{y}_{vt'}, \ t' \in T]$ and $W(Q_N, z_v)$
under the assumption that the empirical distribution
is the population distribution of interest. Specifically,
the treatment-selection probabilities in Table 3.3 were

Table 3.3. Expected welfare and treatment-selection probabilities for alternative empirical success rules.

Covariates	Expected welfare	Treatment-selection probabilities						
		$t = 1$	$t = 2$	$t = 3$	$t = 4$	$t = 5$	$t = 6$	$t = 7$
None	0.718	0	0.003	0	0.028	0.969	0	0
Younger	0.708	0	0.192	0.027	0.145	0.629	0.007	0
Older	—	0.023	0.001	0	0.022	0.954	0.001	0
Blacks	0.742	0	0	0	0	1	0	0
Whites	—	0	0.294	0.024	0.531	0.095	0.056	0
Younger blacks	0.731	0.015	0.042	0.004	0.020	0.917	0.002	0
Older blacks	—	0.010	0	0	0.001	0.989	0	0
Younger whites	—	0	0.264	0.139	0.495	0.06	0.043	0
Older whites	—	0.089	0.257	0.013	0.305	0.227	0.110	0

computed by drawing 5000 pseudo-random samples of size 1275 from the empirical distribution of (covariates, treatments, outcomes) in Table 3.2 and by determining the treatments with maximum empirical success in each pseudo-sample. For example, the entry "0.629" in cell (Younger, $t = 5$) means that when empirical success is measured conditional on age, $t = 5$ maximizes the empirical success rate for younger persons in 0.629 of the pseudo-samples drawn.

In this scenario, the rule that performs best in expected welfare is the one which permits treatment choice to vary with race but not with age: $W_N(Q_N, z_R) = 0.742$. Next best is the rule permitting treatment choice to vary with both race and age: $W_N(Q_N, z_{RA}) = 0.731$. The rule using no covariates performs less well, with $W_N(Q_N, z_\emptyset) = 0.718$. Finally, the rule permitting treatment to vary with age alone yields $W_N(q_N, z_A) = 0.708$. Thus, considering empirical success rules as procedures applied in repeated samples, a physician who conditions treatment choice on race alone can expect to achieve a noticeably higher success rate than does one who treats all patients uniformly or who conditions treatment on age alone.

It is of considerable interest to examine the treatment choice probabilities for the best performing rule. Rule z_R essentially always chooses $t = 5$ for blacks, but selects a wide spread of treatments for whites across repetitions of the sampling process; $t = 4$ has the highest treatment-selection probability (0.531) and $t = 2$ has the second highest (0.294). This feature of the operation of the rule stems from the fact that, for blacks, $t = 5$ substantially outperforms all other treatments in the actual data shown in Table 3.2. For whites, however, Table 3.2 does not show one treatment that is clearly best.

3.3.3 Bounding Expected Welfare and Maximum Regret in Designs with Stratified Random Sampling

The above illustration is instructive, but necessarily limited in its implications. It is easy enough to compute the expected welfare of CES rules in specific cases such as the hypertension RCT. However, it is difficult to characterize in general terms how expected welfare depends on the distribution of treatment response, the conditioning covariates, and the sample size. A particular problem is that treatment-selection probabilities are probabilities that one sample average exceeds other sample averages. Such probabilities generically do not have closed-form expressions.

To make progress, I henceforth focus on the relatively simple case of two treatments, say $T = \{a, b\}$. In this case, it is possible to develop useful closed-form bounds on expected welfare. The upper bound is simple. The highest population welfare attainable by any rule conditioning treatment choice on covariates v is

$$\sum_{\nu \in V} P(v = \nu) \max\{E[u(a) \mid v = \nu], E[u(b) \mid v = \nu]\};$$

hence, $W(z_{Xv}, P, N_{TX})$ and $W(z_v, P, N, q)$ cannot exceed this value. I first develop the lower bound for designs with stratified random sampling and then do the same for those with simple random sampling. In each case, I use the bounds on expected welfare to obtain bounds on maximum regret.

The analysis exploits this large-deviations theorem of Hoeffding (1963, Theorem 2).

Theorem 3.2 (Large-Deviations Theorem (Hoeffding 1963)). *Let* $w_1, w_2, \ldots, w_K$ *be independent real* random variables, with known support bounds

$$[w_{0k}, w_{1k}], \quad k = 1, 2, \ldots, K.$$

Let

$$\bar{w} \equiv \frac{1}{K} \sum_{k=1}^{K} w_k \quad \text{and} \quad \mu \equiv E(\bar{w}).$$

Then, for $d > 0$,

$$\Pr(\bar{w} - \mu \geqslant d) \leqslant \exp\left[-2K^2 d^2 \left\{ \sum_{k=1}^{K} (w_{1k} - w_{0k})^2 \right\}^{-1}\right].$$

The Hoeffding theorem is a powerful result. The only distributional assumption is that the random variables $w_1, w_2, \ldots, w_K$ are independent with known bounds on their supports. The upper bound on $\Pr(\bar{w} - \mu \geqslant d)$ does not depend on the specific distribution of $\bar{w}$, yet converges to zero at exponential rate as either K or d^2 grows. The price for derivation of such a simple large-deviations bound is that it need not be sharp. Hoeffding (1963, Theorem 1) gives tighter bounds on $\Pr(\bar{w} - \mu \geqslant d)$ that hold if $w_1, w_2, \ldots, w_K$ have the same range. However, these bounds are complicated and depend on nuisance parameters.

Bounding Expected Welfare

Proposition 3.3 uses the Hoeffding theorem to bound the expected welfare of a CES rule in a design with stratified sampling. In what follows, recall that

$$u_{0t\xi} \equiv \inf_{y \in Y} u(y, t, \xi) \quad \text{and} \quad u_{1t\xi} \equiv \sup_{y \in Y} u(y, t, \xi).$$

Proposition 3.3. *Let subjects be drawn by stratified random sampling. Let $v(\cdot) : X \to V$ and consider rule z_{Xv}. For $\nu \in V$, define*

$$M_\nu \equiv \max\{E[u(a) \mid v = \nu], E[u(b) \mid v = \nu]\}$$

and

$$\delta_\nu \equiv |E[u(b) \mid v = \nu] - E[u(a) \mid v = \nu]|.$$

Let $L_{t\xi} \equiv (u_{1t\xi} - u_{0t\xi})^2$. Then the expected welfare of rule $z_{X\nu}$ satisfies the inequality

$$\sum_{\nu \in V} P(v = \nu)M_\nu - D(z_{X\nu}, P, N_{TX}) \leqslant W(z_{X\nu}, P, N_{TX})$$

$$\leqslant \sum_{\nu \in V} P(v = \nu)M_\nu,$$

(3.20)

where

$$D(z_{X\nu}, P, N_{TX})$$

$$\equiv \sum_{\nu \in V} P(v = \nu)\delta_\nu \exp\left[-2\delta_\nu^2 \left\{ \sum_{\xi \in X} P(x = \xi \mid v = \nu)^2 \right.\right.$$

$$\left.\left. \times \left(\frac{L_{b\xi}}{N_{b\xi}} + \frac{L_{a\xi}}{N_{a\xi}} \right)^{-1} \right\} \right].$$

(3.21)

Proof. Proposition 1 of Manski (2004) proved this result when $u[y(t), t, x] = y(t)$. The present proposition extends the proof to general welfare functions.

The upper bound in (3.20) is the maximum welfare achievable using covariates v. The task is to prove the lower bound.

Let $\nu \in V$. Let the total sample size be

$$N \equiv \sum_{\xi \in X}(N_{b\xi} + N_{a\xi}).$$

Recall the design-weighted sample average welfare values $\bar{u}_{tX\nu}$, defined earlier. I first write $\bar{u}_{bX\nu} - \bar{u}_{aX\nu}$ as the average of N independent random variables and then apply the Hoeffding theorem. First, observe that

$$\bar{u}_{bX\nu} - \bar{u}_{aX\nu}$$

$$= \sum_{\xi \in X} P(x = \xi \mid v = \nu)\frac{1}{N_{b\xi}} \sum_{j \in N(b,\xi)} u_j$$

$$- \sum_{\xi \in X} P(x = \xi \mid v = \nu)\frac{1}{N_{a\xi}} \sum_{j \in N(a,\xi)} u_j$$

$$= \frac{1}{N} \left\{ \sum_{\xi \in X} \sum_{j \in N(b,\xi)} \left[u_j P(x = \xi \mid v = \nu)\frac{N}{N_{b\xi}} \right] \right.$$

$$\left. + \sum_{\xi \in X} \sum_{j \in N(a,\xi)} \left[-u_j P(x = \xi \mid v = \nu)\frac{N}{N_{a\xi}} \right] \right\}.$$

$$(3.22)$$

Thus, $\bar{u}_{bX\nu} - \bar{u}_{aX\nu}$ averages N independent random variables with ranges

$$\left[P(x = \xi \mid v = \nu)\frac{N}{N_{b\xi}} \right] [u_{0b\xi}, u_{1b\xi}]$$

and

$$\left[P(x = \xi \mid v = \nu)\frac{N}{N_{a\xi}} \right] [-u_{1a\xi}, -u_{0a\xi}],$$

$\xi \in X$.

Suppose that

$$E[u(b) \mid v = \nu] < E[u(a) \mid v = \nu].$$

Then

$$E(\bar{u}_{bX\nu} - \bar{u}_{aX\nu}) = -\delta_\nu.$$

Application of the Hoeffding theorem yields

$$P(\bar{u}_{bX\nu} > \bar{u}_{aX\nu})$$

$$= P(\bar{u}_{bX\nu} - \bar{u}_{aX\nu} + \delta_\nu > \delta_\nu)$$

$$\leqslant \exp\left[-2N^2\delta_\nu^2\right.$$

$$\times\left\{\sum_{\xi\in X}N_{b\xi}\left[(u_{1b\xi}-u_{0b\xi})P(x=\xi\mid v=\nu)\frac{N}{N_{b\xi}}\right]^2\right.$$

$$\left.+N_{a\xi}\left[(u_{1a\xi}-u_{0a\xi})P(x=\xi\mid v=\nu)\frac{N}{N_{a\xi}}\right]^2\right\}^{-1}\right]$$

$$=\exp\left[-2\delta_\nu^2\left\{\sum_{\xi\in X}P(x=\xi\mid v=\nu)^2\right.\right.$$

$$\left.\left.\times\left(\frac{L_{b\xi}}{N_{b\xi}}+\frac{L_{a\xi}}{N_{a\xi}}\right)\right\}^{-1}\right].$$

$$(3.23)$$

Similarly, if

$$E[u(b)\mid v=\nu]>E[u(a)\mid v=\nu],$$

the Hoeffding theorem gives

$$P(\bar{u}_{aX\nu}\geqslant\bar{u}_{bX\nu})$$

$$\leqslant\exp\left[-2\delta_\nu^2\left\{\sum_{\xi\in X}P(x=\xi\mid v=\nu)^2\right.\right.$$

$$\left.\left.\times\left(\frac{L_{b\xi}}{N_{b\xi}}+\frac{L_{a\xi}}{N_{a\xi}}\right)\right\}^{-1}\right].$$

$$(3.24)$$

Inequalities (3.23) and (3.24) hold even when some stratum sample sizes are zero. If either $N_{a\xi}$ or $N_{b\xi}$ equals 0, the formalisms $0^{-1}=\infty$ and $\infty^{-1}=0$ yield

$$\left\{\sum_{\xi\in X}P(x=\xi\mid v=\nu)^2\left(\frac{L_{b\xi}}{N_{b\xi}}+\frac{L_{a\xi}}{N_{a\xi}}\right)\right\}^{-1}=0.$$

To obtain inequality (3.20), we partition V into three regions:

$$V_1 \equiv \{\nu \in V : E[u(b) \mid v = \nu] < E[u(a) \mid v = \nu]\},$$
$$V_2 \equiv \{\nu \in V : E[u(b) \mid v = \nu] > E[u(a) \mid v = \nu]\},$$
$$V_3 \equiv \{\nu \in V : E[u(b) \mid v = \nu] = E[u(a) \mid v = \nu]\}.$$

Then rewrite equation (3.18) as

$$
\begin{aligned}
W(z_{Xv}, & P, N_{TX}) \\
= & \sum_{\nu \in V_1} P(v = \nu)\{E[u(a) \mid v = \nu]P(\bar{u}_{aX\nu} \geqslant \bar{u}_{bX\nu}) \\
& \qquad\qquad + E[u(b) \mid v = \nu]P(\bar{u}_{bX\nu} > \bar{u}_{aX\nu})\} \\
+ & \sum_{\nu \in V_2} P(v = \nu)\{E[u(a) \mid v = \nu]P(\bar{u}_{aX\nu} \geqslant \bar{u}_{bX\nu}) \\
& \qquad\qquad + E[u(b) \mid v = \nu]P(\bar{u}_{bX\nu} > \bar{u}_{aX\nu})\} \\
+ & \sum_{\nu \in V_3} P(v = \nu)\{E[u(a) \mid v = \nu]P(\bar{u}_{aX\nu} \geqslant \bar{u}_{bX\nu}) \\
& \qquad\qquad + E[u(b) \mid v = \nu]P(\bar{u}_{bX\nu} > \bar{u}_{aX\nu})\}.
\end{aligned}
$$
$$(3.18')$$

The first term on the right-hand side of (3.18′) can be no smaller than the expression obtained by setting $P(\bar{u}_{bX\nu} > \bar{u}_{aX\nu})$ at the upper bound obtained in (3.23) and setting $P(\bar{u}_{aX\nu} \geqslant \bar{u}_{bX\nu})$ at its implied lower bound. The lower bound on the second term on the right-hand side of (3.18′) is obtained similarly, by applying (3.24). The third term is constant across all treatment allocations. Placing all three terms on the right-hand side of (3.18′) at their lower bounds yields the lower bound on $W(z_{Xv}, P, N_{TX})$ given in (3.20).   □

The bound on expected welfare obtained in Proposition 3.3 is a closed-form function of the stratum sample sizes N_{TX}, the covariate distribution $P(x)$, and the mean treatment outcomes

$$\{E[u(a) \mid v = \nu], E[u(b) \mid v = \nu], \ \nu \in V\}.$$

The upper bound is the maximum welfare achievable using covariates v. The lower bound differs from this ideal by the nonnegative *finite-sample penalty*

$$D(z_{Xv}, P, N_{TX}),$$

which places an upper bound on the loss in welfare that results from estimating mean treatment outcomes rather than knowing them. The magnitude of the finite-sample penalty decreases with sample size, and it converges to zero at exponential rate if all elements of N_{TX} grow at the same rate.

For each $\nu \in V$, the finite-sample penalty varies nonmonotonically with δ_ν. In particular, it varies as $\delta_\nu \exp(-C_{N\nu}\delta_\nu^2)$, where

$$C_{N\nu} \equiv 2\left\{ \sum_{\xi \in X} P(x = \xi \mid v = \nu)^2 \left(\frac{L_{b\xi}}{N_{b\xi}} + \frac{L_{a\xi}}{N_{a\xi}} \right) \right\}^{-1}.$$

If $\delta_\nu = 0$, there is no finite-sample penalty because both treatments are equally good for persons with covariates ν. As δ_ν increases, the loss in welfare due to an error in treatment selection increases linearly, but the probability of making an error goes to zero at an exponential rate. As a result, the penalty is maximized at

$$\delta_\nu = (2C_{N\nu})^{-1/2}.$$

Inserting the worst-case values

$$[\delta_\nu = (2C_{N\nu})^{-1/2}, \ \nu \in V]$$

into equation (3.21) yields this uniform upper bound on the finite-sample penalty:

$$D(z_{Xv}, P, N_{TX})$$

$$\leqslant \tfrac{1}{2} e^{-1/2} \sum_{\nu \in V} P(v = \nu) \Bigg\{ \sum_{\xi \in X} P(x = \xi \mid v = \nu)^2$$

$$\times \left(\frac{L_{b\xi}}{N_{b\xi}} + \frac{L_{a\xi}}{N_{a\xi}} \right) \Bigg\}^{1/2}.$$

$$(3.25)$$

Bounding Maximum Regret

Proposition 3.3 immediately yields a bound on regret:

$$\sum_{\xi \in X} P(x = \xi) M_\xi - \sum_{\nu \in V} P(v = \nu) M_\nu$$

$$\leqslant U^*(P) - W(z_{Xv}, P, N_{TX})$$

$$\leqslant \sum_{\xi \in X} P(x = \xi) M_\xi - \sum_{\nu \in V} P(v = \nu) M_\nu$$

$$+ D(z_{Xv}, P, N_{TX}).$$

$$(3.26)$$

The lower bound is the benefit of conditioning treatment choice on x rather than v when the distribution of treatment response is known. The upper bound is this quantity plus the finite sample penalty of the rule conditioning on v.

By the law of iterated expectations,

$$E[u(t) \mid v] = \sum_{\xi \in X} E[u(t) \mid x = \xi] P(x = \xi \mid v).$$

Hence, the only unknown quantities in (3.26) are

$$\{E[u(a) \mid x], E[u(b) \mid x]\}.$$

Maximizing the lower and upper bounds on regret in (3.26) over the feasible values of

$$\{E[u(a) \mid x], E[u(b) \mid x]\}$$

yields the following lower and upper bounds on maximum regret:

$$R_{\text{L}v} \leqslant R(z_{Xv}) \leqslant R_{\text{U}}(z_{Xv}), \tag{3.27}$$

where

$$R_{\text{L}v} \equiv \sup_{\gamma \in \Gamma} \sum_{\xi \in X} P(x = \xi)$$

$$\times \max\{E_\gamma[u(a) \mid x = \xi], E_\gamma[u(b) \mid x = \xi]\}$$

$$- \sum_{\nu \in V} P(v = \nu)$$

$$\times \max\{E_\gamma[u(a) \mid v = \nu], E_\gamma[u(b) \mid v = \nu]\},$$

$$R_{\text{U}}(z_{Xv}) \equiv \sup_{\gamma \in \Gamma} \sum_{\xi \in X} P(x = \xi)$$

$$\times \max\{E_\gamma[u(a) \mid x = \xi], E_\gamma[u(b) \mid x = \xi]\}$$

$$- \sum_{\nu \in V} P(v = \nu)$$

$$\times \max\{E_\gamma[u(a) \mid v = \nu], E_\gamma[u(b) \mid v = \nu]\}$$

$$+ \sum_{\nu \in V} P(v = \nu)\delta_{\nu\gamma}$$

$$\times \exp\left[-2\delta_{\nu\gamma}^2\left\{\sum_{\xi \in X} P(x = \xi \mid v = \nu)^2\right.\right.$$

$$\left.\left.\times \left(\frac{L_{b\xi}}{N_{b\xi}} + \frac{L_{a\xi}}{N_{a\xi}}\right)\right\}^{-1}\right],$$

$$\delta_{\nu\gamma} \equiv |E_\gamma[u(b) \mid v = \nu] - E_\gamma[u(a) \mid v = \nu]|,$$

and

$$E_\gamma[u(t) \mid v = \nu] = \sum_{\xi \in X} E_\gamma[u(t) \mid x = \xi]P(x = \xi \mid v = \nu).$$

The lower bound $R_{\text{L}v}$ applies to any rule that conditions treatment choice on covariates v, not only to z_{Xv}. The upper bound $R_{\text{U}}(z_{Xv})$ is specific to this rule.

The bound on maximum regret simplifies in the case of rule z_{Xx}, which conditions treatment choice on all observed covariates. Then $V = X$ and $v(x) = x$, so (3.27) reduces to

$$0 \leqslant R(z_{Xx})$$

$$\leqslant \sup_{\gamma \in \Gamma} \sum_{\xi \in X} P(x = \xi) \delta_{\xi\gamma} \exp\left[-2\delta_{\xi\gamma}^2 \left(\frac{L_{b\xi}}{N_{b\xi}} + \frac{L_{a\xi}}{N_{a\xi}}\right)^{-1}\right].$$

$$(3.28)$$

The upper bound in (3.28) is the supremum of the finite-sample penalty across all feasible states of nature. Suppose that all distributions of treatment response are feasible. Then the derivation of the uniform upper bound on the finite-sample penalty given in (3.25) shows that (3.28) reduces further, to

$$0 \leqslant R(z_{Xx}) \leqslant \tfrac{1}{2} e^{-1/2} \sum_{\xi \in X} P(x = \xi) \left(\frac{L_{b\xi}}{N_{b\xi}} + \frac{L_{a\xi}}{N_{a\xi}}\right)^{1/2}.$$

$$(3.29)$$

Inequalities (3.28) and (3.29) show that rule z_{Xx} is uniformly consistent, and yield lower bounds on its pointwise and uniform rates of convergence. Inequality (3.28) shows that if all elements of N_{TX} grow at the same rate, regret converges to zero at least at an exponential rate in every state of nature. Inequality (3.29) shows that, if all elements of N_{TX} grow at the same rate, maximum regret converges to zero at least with the square root of sample size. Inequality (3.29) also implies that the finite-sample minimax-regret rule is uniformly consistent. Although the form of this rule is unknown, it necessarily has maximum regret no larger than the upper bound in (3.29). Hence, minimax regret converges to zero at a rate no lower than the square root of sample size.

Sufficient Sample Sizes for Productive Use of Covariate Information

Sufficient sample sizes for productive use of covariate information follow immediately from the bounds on maximum regret. Let $v(\cdot) : X \to V$ be a many-to-one mapping of x into a covariate v. The maximum regret of any rule conditioning treatment choice on v must exceed that of rule z_{Xx} if $R_{\mathrm{L}v} > R_{\mathrm{U}}(z_{Xx})$, where $R_{\mathrm{L}v}$ is given in (3.27) and $R_{\mathrm{U}}(z_{Xx})$ in (3.28). The quantity $R_{\mathrm{U}}(z_{Xx})$ is decreasing in each component of the vector N_{TX} of stratum sample sizes. Hence, sufficient sample sizes for conditioning on x to be preferable to conditioning on v are solutions to the problem

$$\min N_{TX} : R_{\mathrm{L}v} > \sup_{\gamma \in \Gamma} \sum_{\xi \in X} P(x = \xi)\delta_{\xi\gamma}$$
$$\times \exp\left[-2\delta_{\xi\gamma}^2 \left(\frac{L_{b\xi}}{N_{b\xi}} + \frac{L_{a\xi}}{N_{a\xi}}\right)^{-1}\right].$$
$$(3.30)$$

Several aspects of this derivation warrant comment. First, with N_{TX} being a vector, problem (3.30) generically has multiple solutions; hence, I refer to sufficient sample sizes (plural). Second, when N_{TX} exceeds a sufficiency boundary, the maximum regret of rule z_{Xx} is smaller than that of *all* rules conditioning treatment choice on v, not just smaller than that of rule z_{Xv}. Third, the sufficiency boundaries provide a sufficient condition for superiority of rule z_{Xx} to rules that condition on v, not a necessary condition. There may not exist any rule conditioning on v whose maximum regret attains the lower bound $R_{\mathrm{L}v}$, and the maximum regret of rule z_{Xx} may be less than $R_{\mathrm{U}}(z_{Xx})$. Fourth, the present analysis does not show that rule z_{Xx} is the best rule conditioning treatment choice on x; there may exist a non-CES rule that is superior to z_{Xx}.

The above discussion compares conditioning on x with conditioning on v. Sufficient sample sizes for other covariate comparisons may be generated in the same manner. Let $v(\cdot) : X \to V$ and $w(\cdot) : X \to W$ be distinct mappings of X into covariates v and w, respectively. Then conditioning on w is necessarily preferable to conditioning on v if N_{TX} is such that $R_{Lv} > R_U(z_{Xw})$, where $R_U(z_{Xw})$ is defined in (3.27).

3.3.4 *Bounding Expected Welfare and Maximum Regret in Designs with Simple Random Sampling*

In designs with simple random sampling, the stratum sample sizes N_{TX} are random rather than fixed. However, the reasoning used to prove Proposition 3.3 continues to apply conditional on any realization of N_{TX}. Hence, Proposition 3.3 provides the "inner loop" for analysis of simple random sampling. Here is the result.

Proposition 3.4. *Let subjects be drawn by simple random sampling. Let* $v(\cdot) : X \to V$ *and consider rule* z_v. *For* $\nu \in V$, *let* $B_{N\nu}$ *denote the binomial distribution* $\boldsymbol{B}[P(v = \nu), N]$. *For* $n = 0, \ldots, N$, *let* B_{nq} *denote the binomial distribution* $\boldsymbol{B}(q_a, n)$, q_a *being the probability with which subjects are assigned to treatment* a. *(If* $n = 0$, *define this distribution to be degenerate with all mass on the value zero.) Let*

$$u_{0t\nu} \equiv \inf_{y \in Y, \xi : v(\xi) = \nu} u(y, t, \xi),$$

$$u_{1t\nu} \equiv \sup_{y \in Y, \xi : v(\xi) = \nu} u(y, t, \xi),$$

and

$$L_{t\nu} \equiv (u_{1t\nu} - u_{0t\nu})^2.$$

Then the expected welfare of rule z_v satisfies the inequality

$$\sum_{\nu \in V} P(v = \nu) M_\nu - D(z_v, P, n, q) \leqslant W(z_v, N, P, q)$$

$$\leqslant \sum_{\nu \in V} P(v = \nu) M_\nu,$$

$$(3.31)$$

where

$$D(z_v, p, N, q) \equiv \sum_{\nu \in V} P(v = \nu) \delta_\nu \sum_{n=0}^{N} \sum_{m=0}^{n} B_{n\nu}(n) B_{nq}(m)$$

$$\times \exp \left\{ - 2\delta_\nu^2 \left[\frac{L_{b\nu}}{(n-m)} + \frac{L_{a\nu}}{m} \right]^{-1} \right\}.$$

$$(3.32)$$

Proof. Proposition 2 of Manski (2004) proved this result when $u[y(t), t, x] = y(t)$. The present proposition extends the proof to general welfare functions. Again, the task is to show the lower bound.

Consider rule z_x, which conditions on all observed covariates. Rule z_x is algebraically the same as rule z_{Xx}, considered earlier. These rules differ only in that the stratum sample sizes N_{TX} are fixed with stratified sampling and are random with simple random sampling. The bounds on treatment-selection probabilities obtained in the proof of Proposition 3.3 hold under simple random sampling, conditional on the realization of N_{TX}. For $\xi \in X$, these bounds are

$$P(\bar{u}_{b\xi} > \bar{u}_{a\xi} \mid N_{TX}) \leqslant \exp \left[- 2\delta_\xi^2 \left(\frac{L_{b\xi}}{N_{b\xi}} + \frac{L_{a\xi}}{N_{a\xi}} \right)^{-1} \right]$$

$$(3.33\,a)$$

if $E[u(b) \mid x = \xi] < E[u(a) \mid x = \xi]$ and

$$P(\bar{u}_{a\xi} \geqslant \bar{u}_{b\xi} \mid N_{TX}) \leqslant \exp\left[-2\delta_\xi^2 \left(\frac{L_{b\xi}}{N_{b\xi}} + \frac{L_{a\xi}}{N_{a\xi}} \right)^{-1} \right]$$
(3.33 b)

if $E[u(b) \mid x = \xi] > E[u(a) \mid x = \xi]$.

The random variable $N_{a\xi} + N_{b\xi}$ is distributed $B_{N\xi}$. Conditional on the event $\{N_{a\xi} + N_{b\xi} = n\}$, $N_{a\xi}$ is distributed B_{nq}. Hence the unconditional treatment-selection probabilities satisfy the inequalities

$$P(\bar{u}_{b\xi} > \bar{u}_{a\xi}) \leqslant \sum_{n=0}^{N} \sum_{m=0}^{n} B_{N\xi}(n) B_{nq}(m)$$
$$\times \exp\left\{ -2\delta_\xi^2 \left[\frac{L_{b\xi}}{n-m} + \frac{L_{a\xi}}{m} \right]^{-1} \right\}$$
(3.34 a)

if $E[u(b) \mid x = \xi] < E[u(a) \mid x = \xi]$ and

$$P(\bar{u}_{a\xi} \geqslant \bar{u}_{b\xi}) \leqslant \sum_{n=0}^{N} \sum_{m=0}^{n} B_{N\xi}(n) B_{nq}(m)$$
$$\times \exp\left\{ -2\delta_\xi^2 \left[\frac{L_{b\xi}}{n-m} + \frac{L_{a\xi}}{m} \right]^{-1} \right\}$$
(3.34 b)

if $E[u(b) \mid x = \xi] > E[u(a) \mid x = \xi]$. The remainder of the proof is the same as that of Proposition 3.3.

Now let $v(\cdot) : X \to V$ be any specified function and consider rule z_v. The same argument as above holds if one applies Proposition 3.3 to a sampling process that stratifies on v rather than on x. $\square$

The bound on expected welfare obtained in Proposition 3.4 is a closed form function of the sample size N, the treatment assignment probabilities q, and the mean outcomes $\{E[u(a) \mid v = \nu], E[u(b) \mid v = \nu], \ \nu \in V\}$. As in Proposition 3.3, the upper bound is the maximum population welfare achievable using covariates v, and the lower bound differs from this ideal by a finite-sample penalty, here $D(z_v, N, P, q)$.

Proposition 3.4 yields this bound on regret:

$$\sum_{\xi \in X} P(x = \xi) M_\xi - \sum_{\nu \in V} P(v = \nu) M_\nu$$

$$\leqslant U^*(P) - W(z_v, P, N, q)$$

$$\leqslant \sum_{\xi \in X} P(x = \xi) M_\xi - \sum_{\nu \in V} P(v = \nu) M_\nu$$

$$+ D(z_v, P, N, q). \tag{3.35}$$

Maximizing over the feasible values of

$$\{E[u(a) \mid x], E[u(b) \mid x]\}$$

yields this bound on maximum regret:

$$R_{\mathrm{L}v} \leqslant R(z_v) \leqslant R_{\mathrm{U}}(z_v), \tag{3.36}$$

where $R_{\mathrm{L}v}$ was defined in (3.27) and

$$R_{\mathrm{U}}(z_v) \equiv \sup_{\gamma \in \Gamma} \sum_{\xi \in X} P(x = \xi)$$

$$\times \max\{E_\gamma[u(a) \mid x = \xi], E_\gamma[u(b) \mid x = \xi]\}$$

$$- \sum_{\nu \in V} P(v = \nu)$$

$$\times \max\{E_\gamma[u(a) \mid v = \nu], E_\gamma[u(b) \mid v = \nu]\}$$

$$+ \sum_{\nu \in V} P(v = \nu) \delta_{\nu\gamma} \sum_{n=0}^{N} \sum_{m=0}^{n} B_{N\nu}(n) B_{nq}(m)$$

$$\times \exp\left\{ -2\delta_{\nu\gamma}^2 \left[\frac{L_{b\xi}}{n - m} + \frac{L_{a\xi}}{m} \right]^{-1} \right\}.$$

Sufficient sample sizes for productive use of covariate information follow from (3.36). Let $v(\cdot) : X \to V$ and $w(\cdot) : X \to W$ be distinct mappings of X into covariates v and w, respectively. Conditioning on w is then necessarily preferable to conditioning on v if N is such that $R_{\mathrm{L}v} > R_{\mathrm{U}}(z_w)$.

3.3.5 Numerical Findings for Binary Covariates

Computation of the bounds on maximum regret is simple and revealing when welfare is the outcome of treatment and covariate x is a binary random variable; thus, let $u[y(t), t, x] = y(t)$ and $X = \{\xi', \xi''\}$. There are then only two CES rules under any experimental design; one rule conditions treatment choice on x and the other does not. A state of nature is a quadruple

$$\{E[y(t) \mid x = \xi];\ t = a, b;\ \xi = \xi', \xi''\}.$$

The present computations suppose that all states of natures are feasible.

The lower bound for the rule that does not condition treatment choice on x is

$$
\begin{aligned}
R_{\mathrm{L}\phi} = \sup_{\gamma \in \Gamma} P(x = \xi') \\
\times \max\{E_\gamma[y(a) \mid x = \xi'], E_\gamma[y(b) \mid x = \xi']\} \\
+ P(x = \xi'') \\
\times \max\{E_\gamma[y(a) \mid x = \xi''], E_\gamma[y(b) \mid x = \xi'']\} \\
- \max\{P(x = \xi')E_\gamma[y(a) \mid x = \xi'] \\
+ P(x = \xi'')E_\gamma[y(a) \mid x = \xi''], \\
P(x = \xi')E_\gamma[y(b) \mid x = \xi'] \\
+ P(x = \xi'')E_\gamma[y(b) \mid x = \xi'']\}, \quad (3.37)
\end{aligned}
$$

where

$$\{E_\gamma[y(t) \mid x = \xi];\ t = a, b;\ \xi = \xi', \xi''\}$$

can take values in the unit hypercube $[0,1]^4$. Without loss of generality, let

$$P(x = \xi') \leqslant P(x = \xi'')$$

and

$$E[y(a) \mid x = \xi'] \leqslant E[y(b) \mid x = \xi'].$$

It can then be shown that a state of nature that solves problem (3.37) is

$$E_\gamma[y(a) \mid x = \xi'] = E_\gamma[y(b) \mid x = \xi''] = 0,$$
$$E_\gamma[y(b) \mid x = \xi'] = 1,$$
$$E_\gamma[y(a) \mid x = \xi''] = P(x = \xi')/P(x = \xi'').$$

Thus, $R_{L\phi} = \min\{P(x = \xi'), P(x = \xi'')\}$.

The upper bounds on maximum regret can be computed numerically. I first consider designs with simple random sampling and then ones with stratified sampling.

Simple Random Sampling

Under simple random sampling, the CES rule conditioning on x is z_x. Table 3.4 computes the upper bound on maximum regret of this rule in designs with equal treatment assignment probabilities ($q = 0.5$) and sample sizes ranging from 1 to 200. Three covariate distributions are considered, with $P(x = \xi') = 0.05, 0.25$, or 0.5; hence, $R_{L\phi} = 0.05, 0.25$, or 0.5, respectively. Table 3.4 shows that the sufficient sample size for productive use of covariate information lies between $N = 100$ and $N = 200$ when $P(x = \xi') = 0.05$, is $N = 15$ when $P(x = \xi') = 0.25$, and is $N = 6$ when $P(x = \xi') = 0.50$.

These numerical findings suggest that prevailing practices in the use of covariate information in treatment choice are too conservative. It is commonly thought that treatment choice should be conditioned on covariates

Table 3.4. Upper bound on maximum regret of rule z_x
under simple random sampling ($q_a = 0.5$).

$P(x = \xi')$	$N = 1$	$N = 2$	$N = 3$	$N = 4$	$N = 5$
0.05	1	0.729	0.510	0.404	0.352
0.25	1	0.862	0.712	0.582	0.503
0.50	1	0.921	0.812	0.699	0.592

	$N = 6$	$N = 7$	$N = 8$	$N = 9$	$N = 10$
0.05	0.318	0.293	0.275	0.258	0.243
0.25	0.456	0.414	0.382	0.355	0.331
0.50	0.496	0.418	0.372	0.340	0.313

	$N = 11$	$N = 12$	$N = 13$	$N = 14$	$N = 15$
0.05	0.235	0.227	0.219	0.212	0.204
0.25	0.309	0.289	0.270	0.256	0.243
0.50	0.295	0.278	0.262	0.252	0.242

	$N = 16$	$N = 17$	$N = 18$	$N = 19$	$N = 20$
0.05	0.197	0.191	0.184	0.180	0.177
0.25	0.233	0.223	0.215	0.207	0.200
0.50	0.233	0.224	0.215	0.207	0.202

	$N = 24$	$N = 28$	$N = 32$	$N = 36$	$N = 40$
0.05	0.166	0.155	0.145	0.135	0.126
0.25	0.177	0.164	0.153	0.144	0.135
0.50	0.184	0.169	0.154	0.143	0.137

	$N = 44$	$N = 48$	$N = 52$	$N = 100$	$N = 200$
0.05	0.117	0.109	0.104	0.076	0.047
0.25	0.128	0.121	0.115	0.083	0.055
0.50	0.132	0.127	0.122	0.078	0.061

only if treatment response varies in a "statistically significant" manner across covariate values. Statistical significance is conventionally taken to mean rejection of the
null hypothesis that mean response is the same across

values of x. This hypothesis is rarely rejected in small samples, so use of covariate information in treatment choice is commonly viewed as imprudent. The findings in Table 3.4 suggest that conditioning treatment choice on covariates is warranted in samples far smaller than those required to show statistically significant differences in treatment response across covariate values.

Numerical findings aside, testing hypotheses is remote in principle from the problem of treatment choice. A planner needs to assess the performance of alternative treatment rules, whether measured by maximum regret or by some other criterion. Hypothesis tests do not address the planner's problem.

Quasi-Optimal Stratified Designs

A stratified design is indexed by the stratum sample sizes N_{TX}. The usual rationale for stratification is to improve statistical precision relative to simple random sampling. A natural way to study treatment choice with stratified data is to fix the overall sample size N and, for each feasible rule, determine the value of N_{TX} that minimizes maximum regret subject to the constraint

$$\sum_{(t,\xi)} N_{t\xi} = N.$$

The present analysis does not yield optimal stratified designs, but it does yield *quasi-optimal* designs that minimize the upper bound on maximum regret. I call these "quasi" optimal designs for two reasons. One is that I restrict attention to CES rules; these designs may not be optimal for other rules. The other is that the criterion considered here is the minimization of the upper bound on maximum regret, not maximum regret itself.

Table 3.5 shows the quasi-optimal designs for the two feasible rules z_{Xx} and $z_{X\phi}$, when N ranges from 1 to 52

Table 3.5. Quasi-optimal stratified random sampling designs. Rule z_{Xx}, $P(x = \xi') = 0.05$.

	$N = 1$	$N = 2$	$N = 3$	$N = 4$
$N_{a\xi'}, N_{b\xi'}$	—	0	0	0
$N_{a\xi''}, N_{b\xi''}$	—	1	$(1, 2)$	2
$R_{\mathrm{U}}(z_{Xx})$	1	0.457	0.403	0.338

	$N = 8$	$N = 12$	$N = 16$	$N = 20$
$N_{a\xi'}, N_{b\xi'}$	0	1	1	2
$N_{a\xi''}, N_{b\xi''}$	4	5	7	8
$R_{\mathrm{U}}(z_{Xx})$	0.250	0.203	0.173	0.154

	$N = 24$	$N = 28$	$N = 32$	$N = 36$
$N_{a\xi'}, N_{b\xi'}$	2	2	2	2
$N_{a\xi''}, N_{b\xi''}$	10	12	14	16
$R_{\mathrm{U}}(z_{Xx})$	0.143	0.133	0.124	0.115

	$N = 40$	$N = 44$	$N = 48$	$N = 52$
$N_{a\xi'}, N_{b\xi'}$	2	2	2	3
$N_{a\xi''}, N_{b\xi''}$	18	20	22	23
$R_{\mathrm{U}}(z_{Xx})$	0.108	0.101	0.094	0.088

and when $P(x = \xi') = 0.05$ or 0.25; the covariate distribution with $P(x = \xi') = 0.5$ is omitted because the quasi-optimal design in this case generically is the equal-shares allocation $\{N_{t\xi} = \frac{1}{4}N;\ t = a, b;\ \xi = \xi', \xi''\}$. The first two rows of each panel of the table show the quasi-optimal stratification, and the third row gives the upper bound on maximum regret. A generic finding is that, for each value of x, equal numbers of subjects should be assigned to each treatment; thus, $N_{a\xi'} = N_{b\xi'}$ and $N_{a\xi''} = N_{b\xi''}$. However, stratum sample sizes being integers, this condition is not strictly implementable when N is odd. The entries $(1, 2)$ for rule z_{Xx} when $N = 3$ show

Table 3.5. (*Cont.*) Rule $z_{X\phi}$, $P(x = \xi') = 0.05$.

	$N = 1$	$N = 2$	$N = 3$	$N = 4$
$N_{a\xi'}, N_{b\xi'}$	—	—	—	1
$N_{a\xi''}, N_{b\xi''}$	—	—	—	1
$R_U(z_{X\phi})$	1	1	1	0.457

	$N = 8$	$N = 12$	$N = 16$	$N = 20$
$N_{a\xi'}, N_{b\xi'}$	1	1	1	1
$N_{a\xi''}, N_{b\xi''}$	3	5	7	9
$R_U(z_{X\phi})$	0.284	0.232	0.204	0.187

	$N = 24$	$N = 28$	$N = 32$	$N = 36$
$N_{a\xi'}, N_{b\xi'}$	1	1	1	1
$N_{a\xi''}, N_{b\xi''}$	11	13	15	17
$R_U(z_{X\phi})$	0.172	0.159	0.152	0.148

	$N = 40$	$N = 44$	$N = 48$	$N = 52$
$N_{a\xi'}, N_{b\xi'}$	1	1	1	1
$N_{a\xi''}, N_{b\xi''}$	19	21	23	25
$R_U(z_{X\phi})$	0.145	0.141	0.137	0.134

that $(N_{a\xi''} = 1$, $N_{b\xi''} = 2)$ and $(N_{a\xi''} = 2$, $N_{b\xi''} = 1)$ are both quasi-optimal in this case of an odd value of N. The blank entries that sometimes appear when $N \leqslant 3$ indicate that all allocations yield the same trivial upper bound on maximum regret, namely 1.

Table 3.5 shows that the quasi-optimal stratification generically draws more subjects with covariate value $x = \xi''$ than with $x = \xi'$. This is unsurprising, given that the two covariate distributions considered in the table have $P(x = \xi') < P(x = \xi'')$. The best designs for rule $z_{X\phi}$ are approximately self-weighting; that is, $N_{t\xi'}/N_{t\xi''} \approx P(x = \xi')/P(x = \xi'')$. This too is unsurprising, given

Table 3.5.   *(Cont.)* Rule z_{Xx}, $P(x = \xi') = 0.25$.

	$N = 1$	$N = 2$	$N = 3$	$N = 4$
$N_{a\xi'}, N_{b\xi'}$	—	0	0	1
$N_{a\xi''}, N_{b\xi''}$	—	1	(1, 2)	1
$R_{\mathrm{U}}(z_{Xx})$	1	0.572	0.529	0.423

	$N = 8$	$N = 12$	$N = 16$	$N = 20$
$N_{a\xi'}, N_{b\xi'}$	1	2	3	3
$N_{a\xi''}, N_{b\xi''}$	3	4	5	7
$R_{\mathrm{U}}(z_{Xx})$	0.293	0.234	0.205	0.182

	$N = 24$	$N = 28$	$N = 32$	$N = 36$
$N_{a\xi'}, N_{b\xi'}$	4	5	6	6
$N_{a\xi''}, N_{b\xi''}$	8	9	10	12
$R_{\mathrm{U}}(z_{Xx})$	0.162	0.153	0.144	0.137

	$N = 40$	$N = 44$	$N = 48$	$N = 52$
$N_{a\xi'}, N_{b\xi'}$	7	8	8	8
$N_{a\xi''}, N_{b\xi''}$	13	14	16	18
$R_{\mathrm{U}}(z_{Xx})$	0.129	0.122	0.116	0.110

that rule $z_{X\phi}$ does not condition treatment choice on the covariate. Perhaps more interesting is the fact that the best designs for rule z_{Xx} generically over-sample subjects with covariate values $x = \xi'$; that is,

$$\frac{N_{t\xi'}}{N_{t\xi''}} \geqslant \frac{P(x = \xi')}{P(x = \xi'')}.$$

The fact that sample sizes are integers makes it difficult to draw conclusions about the degree of over-sampling when $P(x = \xi') = 0.05$. However, it appears that, when $P(x = \xi') = 0.25$, the sampling ratio $N_{t\xi'}/N_{t\xi''} \approx \frac{1}{2}$.

Comparison of Tables 3.4 and 3.5 shows how quasi-optimal stratified random sampling improves treatment

Table 3.5. (*Cont.*) Rule $z_{X\phi}$, $P(x = \xi') = 0.25$.

	$N = 1$	$N = 2$	$N = 3$	$N = 4$
$N_{a\xi'}, N_{b\xi'}$	—	—	—	1
$N_{a\xi''}, N_{b\xi''}$	—	—	—	1
$R_U(z_{X\phi})$	1	1	1	0.585

	$N = 8$	$N = 12$	$N = 16$	$N = 20$
$N_{a\xi'}, N_{b\xi'}$	1	2	2	3
$N_{a\xi''}, N_{b\xi''}$	3	4	6	7
$R_U(z_{X\phi})$	0.464	0.427	0.400	0.385

	$N = 24$	$N = 28$	$N = 32$	$N = 36$
$N_{a\xi'}, N_{b\xi'}$	3	4	4	5
$N_{a\xi''}, N_{b\xi''}$	9	10	12	13
$R_U(z_{X\phi})$	0.374	0.365	0.356	0.348

	$N = 40$	$N = 44$	$N = 48$	$N = 52$
$N_{a\xi'}, N_{b\xi'}$	5	6	6	7
$N_{a\xi''}, N_{b\xi''}$	15	16	18	19
$R_U(z_{X\phi})$	0.342	0.339	0.336	0.333

choice relative to simple random sampling. When N is very small, rule z_{Xx} sometimes substantially outperforms its simple random sampling counterpart z_x. The advantage of stratification declines as N grows but remains nonnegligible throughout the range of sample sizes considered here. The tables indicate that stratification is productive only when one conditions treatment choice on x; rule $z_{X\phi}$ does not outperform its simple random sampling counterpart z_ϕ.

4

The Selection Problem
with Sample Data

This chapter briefly returns to the selection problem. Whereas Chapter 2 assumed that the planner knows the distribution of (covariates, treatments, outcomes) in the study population, I now suppose that he only observes a sample drawn from this population. Thus, the planner must contend with both the selection problem and the necessity of statistical inference from sample to population.

In principle, a planner facing the selection problem with sample data may apply the Wald development of statistical theory described in Section 3.1. He may choose treatments using a Bayes rule as in (3.2), or implement the finite-sample maximin or minimax-regret criteria given in (3.3) and (3.4). However, little is yet known about the analytical properties and computational tractability of these decision criteria when applied to the selection problem with sample data. Hence, this chapter is short.

The analysis that I do provide draws on Manski (2005). I assume that the planner observes the (covariate, treatment, outcome) realizations of N members of the study population. I furthermore assume that, for each $\xi \in X$, the sampling process randomly draws persons with covariates ξ. In this setting, a planner may reasonably apply *sample-analog* treatment rules, which use the empirical distribution $P_N(s, y \mid x = \xi)$ to estimate the population distribution $P(s, y \mid x = \xi)$. Sample-analog rules commonly are computationally tractable and behave well asymptotically. I focus here on treatment choice using the empirical evidence alone.

4.1 Sample-Analog Rules Using the Empirical Evidence Alone

Recall Section 2.1, where we studied treatment choice when a planner observes $P(x, s, y)$ but has no other knowledge of treatment response. A Bayes rule allocated all persons with covariates ξ to a treatment solving (2.11) and the maximin rule allocated all such persons to a treatment solving (2.14). A minimax-regret rule solved (2.15) in general and had the closed-form expression given in Proposition 2.1 when there are two treatments.

The derivations of all these treatment rules used the Law of Iterated Expectations and empirical knowledge of $P(x, s, y)$ to write

$$
\begin{aligned}
E_\gamma[u(t) \mid x = \xi] \\
= E[u(t) \mid x = \xi, \ s = t]P(s = t \mid x = \xi) \\
+ E_\gamma[u(t) \mid x = \xi, \ s \neq t]P(s \neq t \mid x = \xi).
\end{aligned}
\tag{4.1}
$$

Sample analogs of the rules studied in Section 2.1 replace

$$
E[u(t) \mid x = \xi, \ s = t] \quad \text{and} \quad P(s \mid x = \xi)
$$

with

$$
E_N[u(t) \mid x = \xi, \ s = t] \quad \text{and} \quad P_N(s \mid x = \xi).
$$

Thus, for $\xi \in X$, the sample analogs of the Bayes rule and maximin rule solve the problems

$$\max_{t \in T} E_N[u(t) \mid x = \xi, \ s = t] P_N(s = t \mid x = \xi)$$
$$+ q(t, \xi) P_N(s \neq t \mid x = \xi) \quad (4.2)$$

and

$$\max_{t \in T} E_N[u(t) \mid x = \xi, \ s = t] P_N(s = t \mid x = \xi)$$
$$+ u_{0t\xi} P_N(s \neq t \mid x = \xi). \quad (4.3)$$

When there are two treatments, the sample analog of the minimax-regret rule is

$$z^*[b, \xi, P_N(x, s, y)] = \begin{cases} 1 & \text{if } p_{Na\xi}(e_{Na\xi} - u_{0b\xi}) \\ & \quad + p_{Nb\xi}(u_{1a\xi} - e_{Nb\xi}) < 0, \\[2mm] 0 & \text{if } p_{Na\xi}(u_{1b\xi} - e_{Na\xi}) \\ & \quad + p_{Nb\xi}(e_{Nb\xi} - u_{0a\xi}) < 0, \\[2mm] \dfrac{\begin{array}{l} p_{Na\xi}(u_{1b\xi} - e_{Na\xi}) \\ \quad + p_{Nb\xi}(e_{Nb\xi} - u_{0a\xi}) \end{array}}{\begin{array}{l} p_{Na\xi}(u_{1b\xi} - u_{0b\xi}) \\ \quad + p_{Nb\xi}(u_{1a\xi} - u_{0a\xi}) \end{array}} \\ & \text{otherwise,} \end{cases}$$

$$(4.4)$$

where

$$e_{Nt\xi} \equiv E_N[u(t) \mid x = \xi, \ s = t]$$

and

$$p_{Nt\xi} \equiv P_N(s = t \mid x = \xi).$$

These sample-analog rules have two appealing qualities. First, they are as easy to use as the corresponding rules that require knowledge of $P(x, s, y)$. Second, they generically yield the same treatment choices asymptotically as the planner would make given knowledge of

$P(x, s, y)$. This is so because

$$E_N[u(t) \mid x = \xi, \ s = t] \quad \text{and} \quad P_N(s \mid x = \xi)$$

are consistent estimates of

$$E[u(t) \mid x = \xi, \ s = t] \quad \text{and} \quad P(s \mid x = \xi).$$

4.1.1 Sample-Analog Rules and Finite-Sample Rules

Although the sample-analog rules (4.2)–(4.4) behave well asymptotically, they generally are not the same as the Bayes, maximin, and minimax-regret rules using sample data. A Bayesian planner would not use

$$E_N[u(t) \mid x = \xi, \ s = t] \quad \text{and} \quad P_N(s \mid x = \xi)$$

to estimate

$$E[u(t) \mid x = \xi, \ s = t] \quad \text{and} \quad P(s \mid x = \xi).$$

He would place a prior subjective distribution on the feasible states of nature, which include all possible values for the distribution $P(x, s, y)$. He would use the empirical distribution $P_N(x, s, y)$ to update this subjective distribution and then maximize the posterior subjective expected welfare. Finite-sample Bayes rules necessarily depend on the prior subjective distribution placed on Γ. They generally are much more complex to compute than the solutions to (4.2).

A maximin planner would ignore the sample data entirely. We saw in Section 3.2 that a maximin planner who knows the success probability of a status quo treatment, who thinks it feasible that the status quo is superior to an innovation, and who observes the empirical success of the innovation in a finite-sample experiment always chooses the status quo treatment, whatever the experimental findings may be. A maximin planner who faces the selection problem with sample data allocates all persons with covariate ξ to the treatment that solves the problem $\max_{t \in T} u_{0t\xi}$, whatever the sample data may be.

Minimax-regret rules using sample data generally seem complex to analyze or compute. However, a surprisingly simple result emerges when there are two treatments and the logical bounds on welfare are constant across treatments. Then the sample-analog rule (4.4) minimizes finite-sample maximum regret if the sampling process ensures that the sample contains at least one person with each value of x. Proposition 4.1 gives this result.

Proposition 4.1. *Let $T = \{a, b\}$. Let Γ index the states of nature that are feasible without knowledge of $P(x, s, y)$. Let the logical bounds on welfare be constant across treatments, and let $u_{0\xi} \equiv u_{0a\xi} = u_{0b\xi}$ and $u_{1\xi} \equiv u_{1a\xi} = u_{1b\xi}$, $\xi \in X$. Consider any sampling process that, for $\xi \in X$, randomly draws $N_\xi > 0$ members of the study population with covariates ξ. Let $P_N(x, s, y)$ be the empirical distribution of the data. Then*

$$z^*[b, \xi, P_N(x, s, y)]$$
$$= \frac{1}{u_{1\xi} - u_{0\xi}} [p_{Na\xi}(u_{1\xi} - e_{Na\xi}) + p_{Nb\xi}(e_{Nb\xi} - u_{0\xi})]$$

$$(4.5)$$

is a finite-sample minimax-regret rule.

Proof. When the logical bounds on welfare are constant across treatments, Proposition 2.1 showed that the minimax-regret rule using knowledge of $P(x, s, y)$ assigns positive fractions of persons to both treatments, the fraction assigned to treatment b being

$$z^{\mathrm{mr}}(b, \xi) = \frac{1}{u_{1\xi} - u_{0\xi}} [p_{a\xi}(u_{1\xi} - e_{a\xi}) + p_{b\xi}(e_{b\xi} - u_{0\xi})].$$

$$(4.6)$$

When $N_\xi > 0$, the sample-analog rule (4.5) using $P_N(x, s, y)$ in place of $P(x, s, y)$ is well defined and assigns positive fractions of persons to both treatments, the fraction assigned to treatment b being the expression on the right-hand side of (4.5).

The quantity $p_{a\xi}(u_{1\xi} - e_{a\xi}) + p_{b\xi}(e_{b\xi} - u_{0\xi})$ can be written as a sum of two expectations:

$$p_{a\xi}(u_{1\xi} - e_{a\xi}) + p_{b\xi}(e_{b\xi} - u_{0\xi})$$
$$= E\{\mathbf{1}[s = a][u_{1\xi} - u(a)] \mid x = \xi\}$$
$$+ E\{\mathbf{1}[s = b][u(b) - u_{0\xi}] \mid x = \xi\}.$$

Similarly, $p_{Na\xi}(u_{1\xi} - e_{Na\xi}) + p_{Nb\xi}(e_{Nb\xi} - u_{0\xi})$ can be written as the sum of two sample averages:

$$p_{Na\xi}(u_{1\xi} - e_{Na\xi}) + p_{Nb\xi}(e_{Nb\xi} - u_{0\xi})$$
$$= E_N\{\mathbf{1}[s = a][u_{1\xi} - u(a)] \mid x = \xi\}$$
$$+ E_N\{\mathbf{1}[s = b][u(b) - u_{0\xi}] \mid x = \xi\}.$$

Hence, $E\{z^*[b, \xi, P_N(x, s, y)]\} = z^{\mathrm{mr}}(b, \xi)$. This holds whatever values $(e_{a\xi}, p_{a\xi})$ and $(e_{b\xi}, p_{b\xi})$ may take.

The above shows that, whatever values $(e_{a\xi}, p_{a\xi})$ and $(e_{b\xi}, p_{b\xi})$ may take, the finite-sample maximum regret achieved by rule z^*, which uses only knowledge of $P_N(x, s, y)$, equals the maximum regret achieved by rule z^{mr}, which minimizes maximum regret given knowledge of $P(x, s, y)$. Hence, the former rule minimizes finite-sample maximum regret. □

The unbiasedness of $z^*[b, \xi, P_N(x, s, y)]$ as an estimate of $z^{\mathrm{mr}}(b, \xi)$ is a delicate property whose proof uses all the assumptions maintained in Proposition 4.1. Consider the assumption that $N_\xi > 0, \xi \in X$. This ensures that rule z^* always is well defined, a precondition for it to have an expected value. The assumption is not satisfied by simple random sampling, which produces samples having empty covariate cells with positive probability. It is satisfied by the variant of simple random sampling that does not fix the total sample size, but rather continues to draw members of the study population until the sample contains at least one person with each covariate value. It is also satisfied by stratified random sampling processes that fix $(N_\xi > 0, \ \xi \in X)$ and randomly draw members of each stratum.

The proposition shows that z^* is a finite-sample minimax-regret rule, not the unique such rule. Any feasible treatment rule with $E\{z[b, \xi, P_N(x, s, y)]\} = z^{\mathrm{mr}}(b, \xi)$ is finite-sample minimax-regret. A curious implication is that, under the assumptions of this proposition, there is no advantage to large sample size from the finite-sample minimax-regret perspective: observing one randomly drawn person with covariates ξ is as good as observing all such persons. The reason is that Wald's statistical decision theory assumes that the decision maker is risk neutral, concerned only with the expected performance of statistical decision functions across repeated samples.

I am not aware of other applications of the finite-sample minimax-regret criterion in which there exist unbiased estimates of the minimax-regret rule. In particular, unbiased estimates do not exist when the data are from a classical randomized experiment. In this case, the minimax-regret rule assigns all observationally identical persons to the optimal treatment. A finite-sample estimate of this rule is unbiased only if it makes the correct assignment with probability one. No treatment rule using random sample data can be this effective.

References

Angrist, J. 1990. Lifetime earnings and the Vietnam era draft lottery: evidence from social security administrative records. *American Economic Review* 80:313–336.

Angrist, J., G. Imbens, and D. Rubin. 1996. Identification of causal effects using instrumental variables. *Journal of the American Statistical Association* 91:444–455.

Berger, J. 1985. *Statistical decision theory and Bayesian analysis*. New York: Springer.

Bloom, H. 1984. Accounting for no-shows in experimental evaluation designs. *Evaluation Review* 8:225–246.

Blumstein, A., J. Cohen, and D. Nagin (eds). 1978. *Deterrence and incapacitation: estimating the effects of criminal sanctions on crime rates*. Washington, DC: National Academies Press.

Campbell, D. 1984. Can we be scientific in applied social science? *Evaluation Studies Review Annual* 9:26–48.

Campbell, D. and R. Stanley. 1963. *Experimental and quasi-experimental designs for research.* Chicago, IL: Rand McNally.

Chamberlain, G. 2000. Econometrics and decision theory. *Journal of Econometrics* 95:255–283.

Copas, J. 1983. Regression, prediction, and shrinkage. *Journal of the Royal Statistical Society* B 45:311–354.

Crits-Christoph, P. L. Siqueland, J. Blaine, and A. Frank. 1999. Psychosocial treatments for cocaine dependence. *Archives of General Psychiatry* 56:493–502.

DeGroot, M. 1970. *Optimal statistical decisions.* New York: McGraw-Hill.

Droge, B. 1998. Minimax regret analysis of orthogonal series regression estimation: selection versus shrinkage. *Biometrika* 85:631–643.

Dubin, J. and D. Rivers. 1993. Experimental estimates of the impact of wage subsidies. *Journal of Econometrics* 56:219–242.

Ellsberg, D. 1961. Risk, ambiguity, and the savage axioms. *Quarterly Journal of Economics* 75:643–669.

Fisher, L. and L. Moyé. 1999. Carvedilol and the Food and Drug Administration approval process: an introduction. *Controlled Clinical Trials* 20:1–15.

Friedlander, D., D. Greenberg, and P. Robins. 1997. Evaluating government training programs for the economically disadvantaged. *Journal of Economic Literature* 35:1809–1855.

Gueron, J. and E. Pauly. 1991. *From welfare to work*. New York: Russell Sage Foundation.

Halpern, S., J. Karlawish, and J. Berlin. 2002. The continued unethical conduct of underpowered clinical trials. *Journal of the American Medical Association* 288:358–362.

Heckman, J. 1978. Dummy endogenous variables in a simultaneous equation system. *Econometrica* 46:931–959.

Heckman, J. and R. Robb. 1985. Alternative methods for evaluating the impact of interventions. In *Longitudinal analysis of labor market data* (ed. J. Heckman and B. Singer). Cambridge University Press.

Hoeffding, W. 1963. Probability inequalities for sums of bounded random variables. *Journal of the American Statistical Association* 58:13–30.

Imbens, G. and J. Angrist. 1994. Identification and estimation of local average treatment effects. *Econometrica* 62:467–476.

Karlin, S. and H. Rubin. 1956. The theory of decision procedures for distributions with monotone likelihood ratio. *Annals of Mathematical Statistics* 27:272–299.

Kempthorne, P. 1984. Admissible variable-selection procedures when fitting regression models by least squares for prediction. *Biometrika* 71:593–597.

Lehmann, E. 1983. *Theory of point estimation*. New York: Wiley.

Manski, C. 1990. Nonparametric bounds on treatment effects. *American Economic Review Papers and Proceedings* 80:319–323.

References   117

Manski, C. 1995. *Identification problems in the social sciences.* Cambridge, MA: Harvard University Press.

———. 1997. Monotone treatment response. *Econometrica* 65: 1311–1334.

———. 2000. Identification problems and decisions under ambiguity: empirical analysis of treatment response and normative analysis of treatment choice. *Journal of Econometrics* 95:415–442.

———. 2001. Designing programs for heterogeneous populations: the value of covariate information. *American Economic Review Papers and Proceedings* 91:103–106.

———. 2002. Treatment choice under ambiguity induced by inferential problems. *Journal of Statistical Planning and Inference* 105:67–82.

———. 2003. *Partial identification of probability distributions.* New York: Springer.

———. 2004. Statistical treatment rules for heterogeneous populations. *Econometrica* 72:1221–1246.

———. 2005. Minimax-regret treatment choice with missing outcome data. *Journal of Econometrics*, in press.

Manski, C. and D. Nagin. 1998. Bounding disagreements about treatment effects: a case study of sentencing and recidivism. *Sociological Methodology* 28:99–137.

Manski, C. and J. Pepper. 2000. Monotone instrumental variables: with an application to the returns to schooling. *Econometrica* 68:997–1010.

Materson, B., D. Reda, W. Cushman, B. Massie, E. Freis, M. Kochar, R. Hamburger, C. Fye, R. Lakshman, J. Gottdiener, E. Ramirez, and W. Henderson. 1993. Single-drug therapy for hypertension in men: a comparison of six antihypertensive agents with placebo. *The New England Journal of Medicine* 328:914–921.

Materson, B., D. Reda, and W. Cushman. 1995. Department of Veterans Affairs single-drug therapy of hypertension study: revised figures and new data. *American Journal of Hypertension* 8:189–192.

Meinert, C. 1986. *Clinical trials: design, conduct, and analysis.* Oxford University Press.

Mirrlees, J. 1971. An exploration in the theory of optimal income taxation. *Review of Economic Studies* 38:175–208.

National Research Council. 2001. *Informing America's policy on illegal drugs: what we don't know keeps hurting us* (ed. C. Manski, J. Pepper, and C. Petrie). Committee on Data and Research for Policy on Illegal Drugs, Committee on Law and Justice and Committee on National Statistics, Commission on Behavioral and Social Sciences and Education. Washington, DC: National Academy Press.

Polinsky, M. and S. Shavell. 1979. The optimal tradeoff between the probability and magnitude of fines. *American Economic Review* 69:880–891.

———. 2000. The economic theory of public enforcement of law. *Journal of Economic Literature* 38:45–76.

Rosenbaum, P. 1999. Choice as an alternative to control in observational studies. *Statistical Science* 14:259–304.

Samaniego, F. and D. Reneau. 1994. Toward a reconciliation of the Bayesian and frequentist approaches to point estimation. *Journal of the American Statistical Association* 89:947–957.

Savage, L. 1951. The theory of statistical decision. *Journal of the American Statistical Association* 46:55–67.

———. 1954. *The foundations of statistics.* New York: Wiley.

Shavell, S. and L. Weiss. 1979. The optimal payment of unemployment insurance benefits over time. *Journal of Political Economy* 87:1347–1362.

Wald, A. 1950. *Statistical decision functions.* New York: Wiley.

Lightning Source UK Ltd.
Milton Keynes UK
UKHW022319220722
406251UK00003B/294